Journeys across the Pampas and among the Andes

BY FRANCIS BOND HEAD

Edited with an Introduction
by C. Harvey Gardiner

SOUTHERN ILLINOIS UNIVERSITY PRESS
Carbondale and Edwardsville
FEFFER & SIMONS, INC.
London and Amsterdam

LATIN AMERICAN TRAVEL

Contents

	Introduction	vii
I	Pampas and Gauchos	3
II	Buenos Aires	19
III	Modes of Travel	26
IV	San Luis	33
V	The Gold Mines and Lavadcros of La Carolina	36
VI	Mendoza	39
VII	Across the Pampas	43
VIII	The Pampas Indians	65
IX	Across the Great Cordillera	74
X	Santiago	106
XI	The Gold Mines of El Bronce de Petorca	114
XII	The Gold Mine of Caren and the Silver Mine of San Pedro Nolasco	120
XIII	From Santiago to Mendoza	130
XIV	Again the Pampas	133
XV	General Observations Respecting the Working of Mines in South America	155
XVI	Conclusion	167

Introduction

Uncertainty plagued both Argentina and Chile in the mid-1820's. For more than a decade the razing of an old way of life, the Spanish colonial system, had been their chief order of business. However, just as there had been no unanimous condemnation of the practices of centuries past, so no unanimity attended the efforts to create a new order. During the early years of independence men of principle were more than matched by unprincipled men. Unselfish patriots of vision were outnumbered by selfish men whose vision was dimmed by personal greed and a lusting for power.

Those transitional years featured the jealousies that provoked clashes between national and provincial outlooks as well as the suspicions that enveloped ideas and men from abroad. Those were years when military leaders tried to assert their continuing indispensability, and in so doing attempted to block the dominance of the civilian sector in politics. Those were years during which whims of men overrode the rule of law. The 1820's were years when the power structure that included the landed aristocracy, the topmost military men and the foremost church officials reacted to challenges, domestic and foreign, which were affecting the fortunes of Argentina and Chile.

When independence dawned in Chile, the leading figure there was Bernardo O'Higgins. As Supreme Director, O'Higgins introduced a multipronged program which generated both progress and opposition. To cope with serious fiscal problems, he inaugurated a system of tax reform. But simultaneously the devastating earthquake of 1822 dealt the principal port, Valparaiso, and much of the Chilean economy, a frightful setback. Social reform, allied to O'Higgins' ideal of adapting the Chileans to a new political order, was a dominant theme during his era and the strong man's hostility toward many popular social practices spawned widespread resentment. While O'Higgins was trying to put banditry down throughout the land and effect a general calm, the Araucanian Indians challenged the new authority by rising in the south. Matching much of his domestic program, O'Higgins also fostered a progressive foreign outlook, one which included the courting of Britain. But by 1823 the opposition had so mounted that the country was in full rebellion. O'Higgins took the road to exile and much of the remainder of the decade Chile teetered on the brink of chaos. "From 1826 to 1830," the native historian Galdames reminds us, "Chile lived in a state of constant disturbance."

During these years Chile was host to numerous travelers who wrote of their experiences in that land. The earliest citizen of the United States to do so was Samuel Burr Johnston, whose *Letters Written During a Residence of Three Years in Chili* . . . (Erie, 1816) recorded that American printer's stay there. Of the more numerous British contingent, Samuel Haigh (*Sketches of Buenos Ayres, Chile and Peru*, London, 1831) was there in 1817, and Alexander Caldcleugh (*Travels in South America, During the Years 1819–20–21; Containing an Account of the Present State of Brazil, Buenos Ayres, and Chile*, London, 1825) immediately thereafter.

Peter Schmidtmeyer, author of *Travels into Chile, Over the Andes, in the Years 1820 and 1821* . . . (London, 1824), traveled much the same route as Francis Bond Head, and left, in reference to Chile, a most complete economic and geographical description. Pleasantly hopeful accounts of Chile came from the pens of Captain Basil Hall of the Royal Navy (*Extracts from a Journal, Written on the Coasts of Chili, Peru, and Mexico, in the Years 1820, 1821, 1822,* Edinburgh, 1824) and Maria Graham (*Journal of a Residence in Chile, During the Year 1822, and a Voyage from Chile to Brazil in 1823,* London, 1824). John Miers, on the other hand, developed an essentially unfavorable view of Chile in his *Travels in Chile and La Plata . . .* (London, 1826). Quite candidly, Miers declared, "I should lament to hear that any British capitalist, however flattering the offers made to him, should invest his capital in any enterprise upon the soil of Chile," a view which mining supervisor Head shared.

Beyond the Andes, in Argentina, a similar account summarized much of the 1820's: the warfare that won independence yielded to moments of political confusion and the emergence of a strong leader who ended in exile as prelude to another confused period. In Argentina the man about whom the bright hopes centered was Bernardino Rivadavia.

Believing in the rule of law and hoping to promote harmony among diverse political elements, Rivadavia set out to organize the political structure of his country. But his centralized outlook awakened the suspicions and fanned the opposition of the provinces and their ambitious caudillos. The centralist constitution of 1826 sparked rebellion at a moment when the war with Brazil (1825–28) might well have occupied the attention of a more united Argentina. Also deserving of more attention than they received were the following programs of Rivadavia: the stimulation of intellectual life through more schools, libraries, museums, and literary societies; the reduction of the wealth and power of the Roman Catholic Church and the toleration of religious dissent; the support of such humanitarian services as hospitals and orphanages; the promotion of immigration and banking; and the distribution of public lands, which, in retrospect, causes him to be termed "the patron saint of land reform" in Argentina. To all else, Rivadavia added an abiding interest in the successful conduct of Argentine foreign relations. Earlier he had helped to win recognition from England and other powers. He likewise sought commercial ties, and, during the Argentine-Brazilian struggle over Uruguay, he desired the diplomatic intervention of Britain. In July, 1827, the long-gathering opposition induced Rivadavia to resign the presidency and depart his homeland.

In Argentina, as in Chile, the earliest wave of foreigners came principally from England. Many, among them Francis Bond Head, came because of British commercial and investment interests. As might be expected, numerous accounts of Argentine life were soon put before the reader of English. The earliest view of Argentina by a citizen of the United States was set down in *Voyage to South America, Performed by Order of the American Government, in the Years 1817 and 1818, in the Frigate Congress,* which was published in Baltimore in 1819 by Henry M. Brackenridge, the secretary of a trade commission. A year earlier an ex-British officer, Alexander Gillespie, published his *Gleanings and Remarks, Collected During Many Months of Residence at Buenos Aires and Within the Upper Country.* In 1820 Emeric Essex Vidal's *Picturesque Illustrations of Buenos Ayres and Monte Video* ... appeared in London. To this day those water colors constitute a remarkable record of scenes and types. In words, rather than pictures, Thomas George Love's book, *A Five Year's Residence in Buenos Ayres, During the Years 1820 to 1825* ... (London, 1825), focused on precisely the one prominent place slighted by horseman Head. Some of the most painstaking coverage in engineer-botanist John Miers' previously mentioned book related to the Argentina, in both time and space, that Head knew. From Joseph Andrews, a mining representative with opinions which contradicted Head's conclusions, another good view of Argentina of the 1820's is available to us. His *Journey from Buenos Ayres, Through the Provinces of Cordova, Tucuman and Salta to Potosi* ... appeared in London in 1827. The next year J. A. B. Beaumont's *Travels in Buenos Ayres and the Adjacent Provinces of the Rio de la Plata* was also published in London.

More than a century later, Enrique de Gandía, referring to the 1820's, wrote, "La consulta de los viajeros se hace cada día más necesaria." All of the foregoing travel titles contribute to our understanding of that era, but none more so than does the "superb little book" by Francis Bond Head.

Rough Notes Taken During Some Rapid Journeys Across the Pampas and Among the Andes, as Head titled his South American experiences of 1825–26, has been termed a classic by more than one Argentine student of the travel literature of that country. Carlos A. Aldao included Head's volume in the series "La Cultura Argentina" under the title *Las Pampas y los Andes, Notas de Viaje* (Buenos Aires, 1920). In his introduction to that Spanish edition, Aldao reminds his countrymen that Head's detailed writing about the pampas and the gaucho of the 1820's is priceless because contemporary Argentine writers, taking those themes for granted, ignored them in their own writings. Consequently Head is the significant recorder of social history, a traveler whose eyewitness account salvages for posterity a memorable segment of the Argentine past. A generation after Aldao, Enrique Espinoza, writing in 1951, reminded us anew that Head's classic, in part, inspired Sarmiento's masterly *Facundo*.

Whereas most modern travel accounts, regardless of time and place, tend to focus on urban life, Head's volume is different because of its primary emphasis on unsettled regions, on and beyond the frontier. This different kind of account derives from an unusual author. A hard-riding, free spirit, he might have been an unconscious rebel against the town, witness his niggardly treatment of Buenos Aires. Head thrived on meeting nature on her own terms. Even among hardened horsemen, Head is that rare one who rides more than a hundred miles a day for days at a time, sleeps on the ground, drinks questionable water, has a kind word for savage Indians, and whose candor and courage enable him to face loneliness, danger and the unknown with relish. Although he went to Argentina with little Spanish, his limited knowledge of that language never restricted his activity, nor did it reduce his urge to understand a strange way of life. Out of his sympathetic approach to alien ways and scenes came the fuller, more meaningful experience which, put on paper, makes a superior travel book of his Argentine days. Some of the freshness and independence of Head's book is due to his very limited use of hearsay and historical sources.

Based on terse notes rather than a regular journal, Head's writing ranges from the carefully written to the carelessly written, from sound sentences and balanced paragraphs to neither. Indeed, on occasion, it approximates a staccato of naked notes embracing ideas and impressions. Repetitive enough to convey the monotony and immensity of the pampas, the book also moves along fast enough to convey the pounding of hooves on hard, dry turf. It smacks of the rhythms and imagery of poetry and of the rasping of a trip-hammer. Grandeur and sublimity touch the account of his crossing of the Andes; and an earthy naturalness characterizes the graphic descriptions found in his sketches of a curious child, a falling mule, a gifted rider, a barren room. Sometimes he focuses on a simple fact of nature, on other occasions on the timelessness of the nature of man. Mixed, too, are the pathos and humor that fell his lot.

The outdoorsman, the sportsman, and the horseman in Head helped him appreciate the gaucho, as when he wrote, "Vain is the endeavor to explain to him the luxuries and blessings of a more civilized life; his ideas are that the noblest effort of man is to raise himself off the ground and ride instead of walk—that no rich garments or variety of food can atone for the want of a horse; and that the print of the human foot on the ground is in his mind the symbol of uncivilization."

Sometimes the pampas and gaucho are reproduced photographically. "The coarse grass is its sole produce," Head wrote, "and in the summer when it is high, it is beautiful to see the effect which the wind has in passing over this wild expanse of waving grass; the shades between the brown and yellow are beautiful—the scene is placid beyond description—no habitation nor human being is to be seen, unless occasionally the wild and picturesque outline of the gaucho on the horizon—his scarlet poncho streaming horizontally behind him, his balls flying round his head, and as he bends forward toward his prey, his horse straining every nerve; before him is the ostrich he is pursuing, the distance between them gradually diminishing. . . ."

A genuinely toughened rider, the Englishman described himself as follows: "after I had been riding for three or four months, and had lived upon beef and water, I found myself in a condition which I can only describe by saying that I felt no exertion could kill me. Although I constantly arrived so completely exhausted that I could not speak, yet a few hours' sleep upon my saddle, on the ground, always so completely restored me that for a week I could daily be upon my horse before sunrise, could ride till two or three hours after sunset, and have really tired ten and twelve horses a day." Small wonder the horseman is called "Galloping Head."

A by-product of his Argentine experience, Head's enthusiasm for the lasso led him to make such efforts to get that item introduced into the British cavalry that he won a promotion to a majority in 1828.

His contacts with the Pampas Indians were almost nil but Head nevertheless developed considerable admiration for them. Perhaps it was the romantic in him, perhaps, too, his exaggerated affection for the uncivilized red man stemmed from his dislike of the Spanish nation as a civilizing force, as well as from a desire to counteract European ignorance of the original Americans.

The kaleidoscopic presentation of trifles often adds up to considerable understanding, witness such remarks as these: "a beggar on horseback is occasionally seen, with his hat in his hand, singing a psalm in a melancholy tone"; "a number of loads of grass are seen walking about the streets, for the horse that is carrying them is completely hid"; and "The post of Villavicencio, which in all the maps of South America looks so respectable, now consists of a solitary hut without a window, with a bullock's hide for a door, and with very little roof."

On occasion a scene which vividly impressed itself upon Head's consciousness is indelibly conveyed to his reader. Remembering an evening stop at an isolated post hut on the pampas, he wrote, "There was no candlestick, but, with the beef, a little black girl about seven years old, and almost naked, brought in a crooked, brown, tallow candle, which she held in her hand all the time I dined. The little creature had gold earrings and a necklace of red beads. I gave her a large piece of bread, which she ate very slowly, with the most perfect gravity of countenance. As I was dining, I occasionally looked at her. Nothing was white but her eyes and the piece of bread in her mouth. She was watching every mouthful I ate, and her eyes accompanied my fork from the pewter dish to my mouth. With her left hand she was scratching her little woolly head, but nothing moved except her black fingers, and she stood as still as a bronze statue."

Many people, hearing of rich English mining associations, concluded that all Englishmen were rich, a line of thought which Head unhesitatingly challenged. One dispute which called for raw courage he recorded in these words: "I took my pistols off his table, and before I placed them into my belt, I put the muzzle of one of them against his front tooth, and told him very quietly that I would pay him what was proper, but that if he demanded more, I would only pay him with that pistol."

In Chile, despite the weariness of his recent crossing of the Andes and his desire to get on with his inspection of mines, Head lost none of his capacity for converting commonplace scenes to uncommon literary vignettes. "I was now met by," he wrote of his approach to Santiago, "and I overtook, men, women, boys, priests, &c. on horseback, either coming from or going into town, all at a canter, and in very singular dresses. Many of the horses were carrying double, sometimes two giggling girls, sometimes a boy with his grandmother behind him; sometimes three children were cantering along upon one horse, and sometimes two elderly ladies; then a solitary priest with a broad-brimmed white hat and white serge petticoats tucked up all about him, his rosary dangling on his mule's neck, and his pale fat cheeks shaking from the trot. Milk, and strawberries, and watermelons were all at a canter, and several people were carrying fish into the town tied to their stirrups."

Santiago obviously depressed the traveler in more than one respect. "The town is full of priests—the people are consequently indolent and immoral," Head wrote, touching one of his pet peeves, "and I certainly never saw more sad examples of the effects of bad education, or a state of society more deplorable." Quick on the draw, Head occasionally went off half-cocked.

But the major emphasis and best writing concerned Argentina—the pampas and the gaucho. Under the spell of the landscape, he wrote, "The country has no striking features, but it possesses, like all the works of nature, ten thousand beauties. It has also the grandeur and magnificence of space, and I found that the oftener I crossed it, the more charms I discovered in it." Attuned to the riding and freedom of the gaucho, Head was truly sympathetic when he saw the young rider in tears, because "the loss of spurs to a gaucho is a very serious misfortune. They are in fact his only property—the wings upon which he flies for food or amusement." Food and amusement have been the lot of the reader ever since Head put his observations in book form.

Rough Notes Taken During Some Rapid Journeys Across the Pampas and Among the Andes was published initially in London, in September, 1826, by John Murray. A second English edition appeared that same year and the third edition followed in 1828. Meanwhile the only American edition prior to the present one emerged in Boston early in 1827. The fourth London edition is dated 1846 and the last English edition, all of which were published by Murray, appeared in 1861. The Spanish edition of Carlos A. Aldao, published in Buenos Aires in 1920, lacks Memoranda A and B, in which a number of unflattering statements are made about Argentina.

When the book first appeared, Robert Southey, reviewing it for the *Quarterly Review*, wrote of its "all over vivacity and good-humour, with a buoyancy of spirits rarely to be met with. . . ." The unknown reviewer of the work for the *North American Review* declared that "every reader may draw entertainment and instruction from his book." One hundred and forty years later those appreciations of Head's writing are as meaningful as ever.

Francis Bond Head, commonly known as "Galloping Head" because of his narrative of his Argentine adventures, was born January 1, 1793. His early years, indeed until his debt-ridden father lost "The Hermitage" in 1806, were spent at that ancestral place in Kent, not far from Gravesend and Rochester, on the Medway. At fifteen, Francis, small and slender for his age, entered the Royal Military Academy at Woolwich, where his studies included French, classics, mathematics and drawing. Later his writing, bearing a few unobtrusive literary allusions, reflected his education as well as his tastes. Meanwhile, upon graduation, in 1811, he was commissioned a second lieutenant in the Royal Engineers. Almost immediately he sailed for the Mediterranean and his first encounter with alien cultures.

A hurried glimpse of Gibraltar sparked anti-Catholic sentiments in his correspondence but three years of duty at Malta never did identify him closely with the natives. A brief trip to Greece found Head preferring the rugged terrain to the people. After a brief return to England in 1814, the young army officer was ordered to the Continent. During fighting preliminary to the Battle of Waterloo he, already an excellent horseman, had two mounts shot from under him without suffering any injury himself. While in Paris his love of reading prompted the purchase of many books. During the months that followed, Head regularly mixed outdoor physical activity with literary study, spending two hours daily in the saddle—and evoking much praise for his horsemanship—while detailed to duty at Valenciennes.

In the spring of 1816, while on leave in England, he married Julia Valenza Somerville, a sister of Lord Somerville. The newlyweds hurried to France, and the army of occupation. At Cambrai, the next year, Head's eldest child, a son, was born. The following year orders to report to the Castle in Edinburgh terminated the stay on the Continent. In Scotland the monotony of six years of garrison duty was broken by the arrival of three more children. By 1824 Captain Head found it increasingly difficult to support a family of six on his army pay. In addition, he had grown weary of garrison life. That autumn a measure of acclaim came to Head for his masterful removal of towering ruins, some of which were one hundred thirty feet high, in fire-gutted Parliament Square.

Precisely when public attention encouraged him to think further of abandoning his army career, an opportunity to do so presented itself. From a cousin came the suggestion that he turn his attention to mining in South America. Receptive to that proposal, the captain of engineers applied to supervise, at an annual salary of £1,000, the mines of the Rio Plata Mining Association, one of several score of English mining associations then dreaming of El Dorados in the southern Andes. Winning the post, Head retired from the army on half-pay.

The Rio Plata Mining Association, formed in December, 1824, with a paid-up capital of £75,000, boasted a charter based upon a grant by Rivadavia. Like every other new English mining operation, Head's company believed that capital and English miners and mining methods would spell success beyond the Atlantic. Of the choice of men directing the mining operations of those companies, Head once wrote, in explanation, "One of the companies considered that, in order to *guard* their property, no person could be better than an officer of the Guards; other directors resolved that, as *engines* were to be sent out, it would be well to procure officers from the Engineers. Many selected officers from the artillery, because they heard *gunpowder* was to be required for the Mines." (Sydney Jackman, *Galloping Head: the Life of the Right Honourable Sir Francis Bond Head*, London, 1958, p.41.)

Ever a man of action, Head quickly packed and sailed for Argentina, accompanied by his family, a French assayer, two captains of Cornish mines, and three English miners. Landing late in July, 1825, in Buenos Aires, whence he had been preceded by a contingent of German miners, he settled his family on the outskirts of that port city. Almost immediately he set out for the mines with his corps of experts. The mines assigned the Rio Plata Mining Association were far removed from the river basin of that name. Some were situated north of San Luis and others were northwest of Mendoza, near Upsallata in west central Argentina. Head, the horseman turned mine supervisor, had thousands of land miles ahead of him in his tour of inspection.

Armed with official papers, letters of introduction, boundless personal enthusiasm and energy, and a limited command of Spanish, the Englishman rode west across the pampas. At times astride a horse and on other occasions inside a coach, he went to the gold mines near San Luis and the silver mines of Upsallata, all of which, improperly assigned by Rivadavia to the Rio Plata Mining Association, had been disposed to rival companies. Whether calling upon governors and other officials or descending mine shafts, Head was racing against time. Leaving his party at Mendoza, he galloped nearly one thousand miles to Buenos Aires in the space of eight days. There he received letters which required his immediate departure for Chile.

After a third crossing of the pampas, the supervisor

rejoined his men in Mendoza, crossed the Andes, glimpsed Santiago, and investigated the gold mines of El Bronce de Petorca and Caren to the north of the Chilean capital. Then, turning south of that city, his survey embraced the tortuous setting of the silver mine of San Pedro Nolasco. Returning eastward across the Andes, the dynamic Englishman savored the east-west extension of the pampas a fourth time as he and his party returned to Buenos Aires.

Study of the successive mines—their physical settings, available labor force, equipment needs, transportation costs, and much else—convinced Head that the English mining associations were a colossal mistake, "that both the formation of these Companies, and their failure, have proceeded from one cause—our Ignorance of the country which was to be the field of speculation."

Nevertheless, while amassing the data which quickly returned him to England with a mining report couched in the negative, Head had tasted, and enjoyed, those areas of Argentine and Chilean life which made pleasantly insistent his recording them for English readers. Fruits of the enjoyment he had known on the pampas and among the mountains of South America were the staccato-like notes which he had jotted down at fondas, post huts, river crossings, and other unlikely places.

Reestablished in England, Head penned two versions of his South American experience. By late summer of 1826 his personal narrative, his *Rough Notes Taken During Some Rapid Journeys Across the Pampas and Among the Andes*, appeared in London. The one hundred guineas which publisher John Murray paid the author for that manuscript helped Head to determine upon a literary career. In February, 1827, the same publisher issued Head's *Reports Relating to the Failure of the Rio Plata Mining Association*. It created a furor and closed Head's career as a mining supervisor.

Intermittently, across the next fifty years, Francis Bond Head was identified with writing and publishing, and especially with the house of Murray. As a regular contributor to the *Quarterly Review*, he demonstrated remarkable versatility and literary cleverness. Indeed he seemed at home with almost any subject, ranging, in the words of Samuel Smiles, "from Rapid Rides across the Pampas, to Stokers and Pokers on a Railway; from Mining to Waterloo; from the Red Man to the Printer's Devil; from Steam to Electricity and the Post Office; from governing Paupers to governing a Province."

Some of Head's books, as his *Bubbles from the Brunnens of Nassau*, won the popularity evident in their numerous printings and editions. After service, in 1834, as an assistant poor law commissioner in Kent, he wrote a blistering account of the abuses of the system. Another political appointment, that of Lieutenant Governor of Upper Canada in the mid-1830's, found the politically inexperienced but able Head in the midst of provincial jealousies. With a loyal militia he quelled the insurrection of 1837 which, in the much publicized "Caroline" affair, touched the United States and some of its citizens. Needless to say, Head's Canadian experience also provided grist for his literary mill.

Created a baronet during his service in Canada, Head, upon his return to England in 1838, divorced himself from public life, except for membership in the privy council much later, in 1867.

Meanwhile he rode his horses and pushed his pen. Active and well-preserved to an advanced age, he still was riding to hounds at the age of seventy-five. Death came in his eighty-sixth year, on March 23, 1879. Any assessment of his literary career, many of the products of which border on the labors of a hack, must insist that his first effort, that lively record of rough moments on a rugged South American landscape which adds up to an imperishably fine account of the pampas and gaucho, was his best book.

The editor's role, in addition to this introduction, has included the following: the abbreviation of the title and the restyling of the chapter headings; the consolidation or subdivision of chapters along lines of thematic unity; the deletion of the original introduction; the incorporation of the expository footnotes into the text; the correction of typographical errors and misspelled Spanish words; the modernization and Americanization of some spelling (e.g. wagon not waggon, center not centre); the elimination of repetitive explanations of foreign terms; minor changes in capitalization and punctuation in terms of modern practice; and occasionally the division of overly long sentences. The body of the original work, however, remains complete in this edition, which is the American 1827 edition, supplemented with the paragraphs added to the English edition of 1846.

The Oaks   C. HARVEY GARDINER
Murphysboro, Illinois
March 1, 1967

JOURNEYS ACROSS THE PAMPAS
AND AMONG THE ANDES

Pampas and Gauchos

The mountains of the Andes run about north and south through the whole of South America, and they are consequently nearly parallel to the two shores of the Pacific and the Atlantic Oceans, dividing the country between them into two unequal parts, each bounded by an ocean and by the cordillera.

It would at first be expected that these twin countries, separated only by a range of mountains, should have a great resemblance to each other; but variety is the attribute of Omnipotence, and nature has granted to these two countries a difference of climate and geological construction which is very remarkable.

From the tops of the Andes she supplies both of them with water; by the gradual melting of the snow they are both irrigated exactly in proportion to their wants; and vegetation, instead of being exhausted by the burning sun of summer, is thus nourished and supported by the very heat which threatened to destroy it.

The water, however, which flows through Chile towards the Pacific, is confined in its whole course, and forces its way through a country as mountainous as the highlands of Scotland or Switzerland. The water which descends from the east side of the cordillera meanders through a vast plain nine hundred miles in breadth; and at the top of the Andes it is singular to observe on the right and left the snow of one storm, part of which is decreed to rush into the Pacific, while the other is to add to the distant waves of the Atlantic.

The great plain, or pampas, on the east of the cordillera, is about nine hundred miles in breadth, and the part which I have visited, though under the same latitude, is divided into regions of different climate and produce.

3

On leaving Buenos Aires, the first of these regions is covered for one hundred and eighty miles with clover and thistles; the second region, which extends for four hundred and fifty miles, produces long grass; and the third region, which reaches the base of the cordillera, is a grove of low trees and shrubs. The second and third of these regions have nearly the same appearance throughout the year, for the trees and shrubs are evergreens, and the immense plain of grass only changes its color from green to brown; but the first region varies with the four seasons of the year in a most extraordinary manner. In winter, the leaves of the thistles are large and luxuriant, and the whole surface of the country has the rough appearance of a turnip field. The clover in this season is extremely rich and strong; and the sight of the wild cattle grazing in full liberty on such pasture is very beautiful. In spring, the clover has vanished, the leaves of the thistles have extended along the ground, and the country still looks like a rough crop of turnips. In less than a month the change is most extraordinary; the whole region becomes a luxuriant wood of enormous thistles, which have suddenly shot up to a height of ten or eleven feet, and are all in full bloom. The road or path is hemmed in on both sides; the view is completely obstructed; not an animal is to be seen; and the stems of the thistles are so close to each other, and so strong, that, independent of the prickles with which they are armed, they form an impenetrable barrier. The sudden growth of these plants is quite astonishing; and though it would be an unusual misfortune in military history, yet it is really possible, that an invading army, unacquainted with this country, might be imprisoned by these thistles before they had time to escape from them. The summer is not over before the scene undergoes another rapid change: the thistles suddenly lose their sap and verdure, their heads droop, the leaves shrink and fade, the stems become black and dead, and they remain rattling with the breeze one against another, until the violence of the pampero or hurricane levels them with the ground, where they rapidly decompose and disappear—the clover rushes up, and the scene is again verdant.

Although a few individuals are either scattered along the path, which traverses these vast plains, or are living together in small groups, yet the general state of the country is the same as it has been since the first year of its creation. The whole country bears the noble stamp of an Omnipotent Creator, and it is impossible for anyone to ride through it, without feelings which it is very pleasing to entertain; for although in all countries "the heavens declare the glory of God, and the firmament showeth his handy work," yet the surface of populous countries affords generally the insipid produce of man's labor; it is an easy error to consider that he who has tilled the ground, and has sown the seed, is the author of his crop, and, therefore, those who are accustomed to see the confused produce, which in populous and cultivated countries is the effect of leaving ground to itself, are at first surprised in the pampas, to observe the regularity and beauty of the vegetable world when left to the wise arrangements of nature.

The vast region of grass in the pampas for four hundred and fifty miles is without a weed, and the region of wood is equally extraordinary. The trees are not crowded, but in their growth such beautiful order is observed that one may gallop between them in every direction. The young trees are rising up, others are flourishing in full vigor, and it is for some time that one looks in vain for those which in the great system of succession must necessarily somewhere or other be sinking towards decay. They are at last discovered, but their fate is not allowed to disfigure the general cheerfulness of the scene, and they are seen enjoying what may literally be termed a green old age. The extremities of their branches break off as they die, and when nothing is left but the hollow trunk, it is still covered with twigs and leaves, and at last is gradually concealed from view by the young shoot, which, born under the shelter of its branches, now rises rapidly above it, and conceals its decay. A few places are met with which have been burnt by accident, and the black desolate spot, covered with the charred trunks of trees, resembles a scene in the human world of pestilence or war. But the fire is scarcely extinct, when the surrounding trees all seem to spread their branches towards each other, and young shrubs are seen rising out of the ground, while the sapless trunks are evidently mouldering into dust.

The rivers all preserve their course, and the whole country is in such beautiful order, that if cities and millions of inhabitants could suddenly be planted at proper intervals and situations, the people would have nothing to do but to drive out their cattle to graze, and, without any previous preparation, to plough whatever quantity of ground their wants might require.

The climate of the pampas is subject to a great difference of temperature in winter and summer, though the gradual changes are very regular. The winter is about as cold as our month of November, and the ground at sunrise is always covered with white frost, but the ice is seldom more than one-tenth of an inch thick. In summer the sun is very oppressively hot, and its force is acknowledged by every living animal. The wild horses and cattle are evidently exhausted by it, and the siesta seems to be a repose which is natural and necessary to all. The middle of the day is not a moment for work, and as the mornings are cool, the latter are evidently best adapted for labor, and the former for repose.

The difference between the atmosphere of Mendoza, San Luis, and Buenos Aires, which are all nearly under the same latitude, is very extraordinary: in the two former, or in the regions of wood and grass, the air is extremely dry; there is no dew at night; in the hottest weather there is apparently very little perspiration and the dead animals lie on the plain dried up in their skins, so that occasionally I have at first scarcely been able to determine whether they were alive or dead. But in the province of Buenos Aires, or in the region of thistles and clover, vegetation clearly announces the humidity of the climate. In sleeping out at night I have found my poncho (or rug) nearly wet through with the dew, and my boots so damp that I could scarcely draw them on. The dead animals on the plain are in a rapid state of putrefaction. On arriving at Buenos Aires the walls of the houses are so damp that it is cheerless to enter them; and sugar, as also all deliquescent salts, are there found nearly dissolved. This dampness, however, does not appear to be unhealthy. The gauchos and even travelers sleep on the ground, and the inhabitants of Buenos Aires live in their damp houses without complaining of rheumatism, or being at all subject to cold; and they certainly have the appearance of being rather more robust and healthy than those who live in the drier regions. However, the whole of the pampas may be said to enjoy as beautiful and as salubrious an atmosphere as the most healthy parts of Greece and Italy, and without being subject to malaria.

The only irregularity in the climate is the pampero or southwest wind, which, generated by the cold air of the Andes, rushes over these vast plains with a velocity and a violence which it is almost impossible to withstand. But this rapid circulation of the atmosphere has very beneficial effects, and the weather, after one of these tempests, is always particularly healthy and agreeable.

The south part of the pampas is inhabited by the Pampas Indians, who have no fixed abode, but wander from place to place as the herbage around them becomes consumed by their cattle. The north part of the pampas, and the rest of the provinces of the Río de la Plata, are inhabited by a few straggling individuals, and a few small groups of people, who live together only because they were born together. Their history is really very curious.

As soon as by the fall of the Spaniards their independence was established, and they became free, the attention of many individuals of the provinces of la Plata was directed towards the due constitution of governments which might maintain the freedom that was gained, encourage population, and gradually embellish the surface of a most interesting and beautiful country with the arts, manufactures, and sciences, which had hitherto been denied it; but the singular situation of the country presented very serious difficulties.

Although immense regions of rich land lay uncultivated and unowned, yet something had been done. Small towns and establishments (originally chosen for mining purposes), five hundred and seven hundred miles distant from one another, were thinly scattered over this vast extent of country; and thus a skeleton map of civilization had been traced, which the narrow interests of every individual naturally supported.

But although a foundation was thus laid, the building plan of the Spaniards was missing. It had been destroyed in the war, and all that was known of it was, that it was for purposes which were not applicable to the great political system which should now be adopted.

It was soon perceived that the provinces of the Río de la Plata were without a harbor; that the town of Buenos Aires was badly situated; and as the narrow policy of Spain had forbidden the planting of the olive and the grape, the spots which were best adapted to the natural produce of the country had been neglected: while for mining, and other purposes connected with the Spanish system, towns had been built in the most remote and impracticable situations; and men found themselves living together in groups they knew not why, under circumstances which threw a damp over exertion, and under difficulties which it appeared hopeless to encounter.

Their situation was, and still is, very lamentable. The climate easily affords them the few necessaries of life. Away from all practicable communication with the civilized world, they are unable to partake of the improvements of the age, or to shake off the errors and the disadvantages of a bad political education. They have not the moral means of improving their country, or of being improved by it; and oppressed by these and other disadvantages, they naturally yield to habits of indolence and inactivity. The town, or rather the secluded village, in which they live, is generally the seat of government of the province, and but too often affords a sad political picture.

People who, although they are now free, were brought up under the dark tyranny of the Spanish government, with the narrow prejudices which even in populous countries exist among the inhabitants of small communities, and with little or no education, are called upon to elect a governor, and to establish a junta, to regulate the affairs of their own province, and to send a deputy to a distant national assembly at Buenos Aires. The consequence (as I have witnessed) is what might naturally be expected. The election of the governor is seldom unanimous, and he is scarcely seated before he is overturned, in a manner which, to one accustomed to governments on a larger scale, appears childish and ridiculous.

In more than one province the governor is exceedingly tyrannical: in the others, the governor and the junta appear to act for the interests of their own province; but their funds are so small, and the internal jealousies they have to encounter so great, that they meet with continual difficulties; and with respect to acting for the national interest, the thing is impossible. How can it be expected that people of very slender incomes, and in very small insulated societies, will forget their own narrow interests for the general welfare of their country? It is really against nature, for what is politically termed their country is such an immense space that it must necessarily become the future seat of many different communities of men; and if these communities, however enlightened they may become, will never be able to conquer that feeling which endears them to their homes, or the centrifugal prejudice with which they view their neighbors, how can it be expected that a feeble government and a few inhabitants can do what civilization has not yet been able to perform; or that the political infant will not betray those frailties which his manhood will be incapable of overcoming. And the fact is, that each province does view its neighboring one with jealousy, and as I have traveled through the country, I have invariably found that *mala gente* is the general appellation which the people give to those of the adjoining province, and that they, as well as the inhabitants of the towns, are all jealous of the power and influence of the town of Buenos Aires; and when it is explained that the policy of Buenos Aires is to break the power of the monks and priests, and that these people have still very great influence in most of the distant provinces, and that the maritime interest of Buenos Aires is necessarily often at variance with that of the inland provinces, it will be perceived how forcibly this jealousy is likely to act.

The situation of the gaucho is naturally independent of the political troubles which engross the attention of the inhabitants of the towns. The population or number of these gauchos is very small, and at great distances from each other: they are scattered here and there over the face of the country. Many of these people are descended from the best families in Spain; they possess good manners, and often very noble sentiments: the life they lead is very interesting—they generally inhabit the hut in which they were born, and in which their fathers and grandfathers lived before them, although it appears to the stranger to possess few of the allurements of *dulce domum*. The huts are built in the same simple form; for although luxury has ten thousand plans and elevations for the frail abode of its more frail tenant, yet the hut in all countries is the same, and therefore there is no difference between that of the South American gaucho, and the Highlander of Scotland, excepting that the former is built of mud, and covered with long yellow grass, while the other is formed of stones, and thatched with heather. The materials of both are the immediate produce of the soil, and both are so blended in color with the face of the country, that it is often difficult to distinguish them; and as the pace at which one gallops in South America is rapid, and the country flat, one scarcely discovers the dwelling before one is at the door.

The corral is about fifty or one hundred yards from the hut, and is a circle of about thirty yards in diameter, enclosed by a number of strong rough posts, the ends of which are struck into the ground. Upon these posts are generally a number of idle-looking vultures or hawks. The hawks are very tame, and they are seldom to be seen except at the huts; but occasionally they have followed me for many leagues, keeping just before me, and with their round black eyes gazing intently on my face, which I fancied attracted their notice from being burnt by the sun, and I literally often thought they were a little inclined to taste it. They are constantly in the habit of attacking the horses and mules who have sore backs; and I have often observed these birds hovering about six inches above them. It is curious to compare the countenance of the two animals. The hawk, with his head bent downwards, and his eye earnestly fixed upon the wound: the mule with his back crouched down, his ears lying back, whisking his tail, afraid to eat, and apparently not knowing whether to rear or kick. The ground around the hut and corral is covered with bones and carcasses of horses, bullocks' horns, wool, &c., which give it the smell and appearance of an ill-kept dog-kennel in England.

The hut consists generally of one room, in which all the family live, boys, girls, men, women, and children, all huddled together. The kitchen is a detached shed a few yards off: there are always holes, both in the walls and in the roof of the hut, which one at first considers as singular marks of the indolence of the people. In the summer this abode is so filled with fleas and vinchucas (which are bugs as large as black beetles) that the whole family sleep on the ground in front of their dwelling; and when the traveler arrives at night, and after unsaddling his horse walks among this sleeping community, he may place the saddle or recado on which he is to sleep close to the companion most suited to his fancy:—an admirer of innocence may lie down by the side of a sleeping infant; a melancholy man may slumber near an old black woman; and one who admires the fairer beauties of creation may very demurely lay his head on his saddle, within a few inches of the idol he adores. However, there is nothing to assist the judgment but the bare feet and ankles of all the slumbering group, for their heads and bodies are covered and disguised by the skin and poncho which cover them.

In winter the people sleep in the hut, and the scene is a very singular one. As soon as the traveler's supper is ready, the great iron spit on which the beef has been roasted is brought into the hut, and the point is struck into the ground: the gaucho then offers his guest the skeleton of a horse's head, and he and several of the family, on similar seats, sit round the spit, from which with their long knives they cut very large mouthfuls. (When first I lived with the gauchos, I could not conceive how they possibly managed to eat so quickly meat which I found so unusually tough, but an old gaucho told me it was because I did not know what parts to select, and he immediately cut me a large piece which was quite tender. I always afterwards begged the gauchos to help me, and they generally smiled at my having discovered the secret.)

The hut is lighted by a feeble lamp, made of bullock's tallow; and it is warmed by a fire of charcoal: on the walls of the hut are hung, upon bones, two or three bridles and spurs, and several lassos and balls: on the ground are several dark-looking heaps, which one can never clearly distinguish; on sitting down upon these when tired, I have often heard a child scream underneath me, and have occasionally been mildly asked by a young woman, what I wanted?—at other times up has jumped an immense dog! While I was once warming my hands at the fire of charcoal, seated on a horse's head, looking at the black roof in a reverie, and fancying I was quite by myself, I felt something touch me, and saw two naked black children leaning over the charcoal in the attitude of two toads: they had crept out from under some of the ponchos, and

I afterwards found that many other persons, as well as some hens sitting upon eggs, were also in the hut. In sleeping in these huts, the cock has often hopped upon my back to crow in the morning; however, as soon as it is daylight, everybody gets up.

The life of the gaucho is very interesting. Born in the rude hut, the infant gaucho receives little attention, but is left to swing from the roof in a bullock's hide, the corners of which are drawn towards each other by four strips of hide. In the first year of his life he crawls about without clothes, and I have more than once seen a mother give a child of this age a sharp knife, a foot long, to play with. As soon as he walks, his infantine amusements are those which prepare him for the occupations of his future life: with a lasso made of twine he tries to catch little birds, or the dogs, as they walk in and out of the hut. By the time he is four years old he is on horseback, and immediately becomes useful by assisting to drive the cattle into the corral. The manner in which these children ride is quite extraordinary: if a horse tries to escape from the flock which are driven towards the corral, I have frequently seen a child pursue him, overtake him, and then bring him back, flogging him the whole way; in vain the creature tries to dodge and escape from him, for the child turns with him, and always keeps close to him; and it is a curious fact, which I have often observed, that a mounted horse is always able to overtake a loose one.

His amusements and his occupations soon become more manly—careless of the vizcacheras (the holes of an animal called the vizcacha) which undermine the plains, and which are very dangerous, he gallops after the ostrich, the gama, the lion, and the tiger; he catches them with his balls: and with his lasso he daily assists in catching the wild cattle, and in dragging them to the hut either for slaughter, or to be marked. He breaks in the young horses in the manner which I have described, and in these occupations is often away from his hut many days, changing his horse as soon as the animal is tired, and sleeping on the ground. As his constant food is beef and water, his constitution is so strong that he is able to endure great fatigue; and the distances he will ride, and the number of hours that he will remain on horseback, would hardly be credited. The unrestrained freedom of such a life he fully appreciates; and, unacquainted with subjection of any sort, his mind is often filled with sentiments of liberty which are as noble as they are harmless, although they of course partake of the wild habits of his life. Vain is the endeavor to explain to him the luxuries and blessings of a more civilized life; his ideas are that the noblest effort of man is to raise himself off the ground and ride instead of walk—that no rich garments or variety of food can atone for the want of a horse—and that the print of the human foot on the ground is in his mind the symbol of uncivilization.

The gaucho has by many people been accused of indolence; those who visit his hut find him at the door with his arms folded, and his poncho thrown over his left shoulder like a Spanish cloak; his hut is in holes, and would evidently be made more comfortable by a few hours' labor: in a beautiful climate, he is without fruit or vegetables; surrounded by cattle, he is often without milk; he lives without bread, and he has no food but beef and water, and therefore those who contrast his life with that of the English peasant accuse him of indolence; but the comparison is inapplicable, and the accusation unjust; and anyone who will live with the gaucho, and will follow him through his exertions, will find that he is anything but indolent, and his surprise will be that he is able to continue a life of so much fatigue. It is true that the gaucho has no luxuries, but the great feature of his character is that he is a person without wants: accustomed constantly to live in the open air, and to sleep on the ground, he does not consider that a few holes in his hut deprive it of its comfort. It is not that he does not like the taste of milk, but he prefers being without it to the everyday occupation of going in search of it. He might, it is true, make cheese, and sell it for money, but if he has got a good saddle and good spurs, he does not consider that money has much value: in fact, he is contented with his lot; and when one reflects that, in the increasing series of human luxuries, there is no point that produces contentment, one cannot but feel that there is perhaps as much philosophy as folly in the gaucho's determination to exist without wants; and the life he leads is certainly more noble than if he was slaving from morning till night to get other food for his body or other garments to cover it. It is true he is of little service to the great cause of civilization, which it is the duty of every rational being to promote; but an humble individual, living by himself in a boundless plain, cannot introduce into the vast uninhabited regions which surround him either arts or sciences: he may, therefore, without blame be permitted to leave them as he found them, and as they must remain, until population, which will create wants, devises the means of supplying them.

The character of the gaucho is often very estimable; he is always hospitable—at his hut the traveler will always find a friendly welcome, and he will often be received with a natural dignity of manner which is very remarkable, and which he scarcely expects to meet with in such a miserable-looking hovel. On entering the hut, the gaucho has constantly risen to offer me his seat, which I have declined, and many compliments and bows have passed, until I have accepted his offer, which is the skeleton of a horse's head. It is curious to see them invariably take off their hats to each other as they enter into a room which has no window, a bullock's hide for a door, and but little roof.

The habits of the women are very curious: they have literally nothing to do; the great plains which surround them offer them no motive to walk, they seldom ride, and *their* lives certainly are very indolent and inactive. They have all, however, families, whether married or not; and once when I inquired of a young woman employed in nursing a very pretty child, who was the father of the "criatura," she replied, "Quién sabe?"

The religion which is professed throughout the provinces of the Río de la Plata is the Roman Catholic, but it is very different in different places. During the reign of the Spaniards, the monks and priests had everywhere very great influence; and the dimensions of the churches at Buenos Aires, Luján, Mendoza, &c., show the power and riches they possessed, and the greedy ambition which governed them. It is a sad picture to see a number of small, wretched-looking huts surrounding a church whose haughty elevation is altogether inapplicable to the humility of the Christian religion; and one cannot help comparing it with the quiet village church of England, whose exterior and interior tends rather to humble the feelings of the arrogant and proud, while to the peasant it has the cheerful appearance of his own home. When it is considered that the churches in South America were principally built for the conversion of the Indians to the Christian faith, it is melancholy to think that the priests should have attempted, by the pomp of their temples, and by the mummery of candles, and pictures, and images, to have done what by reason, and kindness, and humility, would surely have been better performed. But their secret object was to extort money; and as it is always easier to attract a crowd of people by bad passions than by good, they therefore made their temples as attractive as possible, and men were called to see and to admire, instead of to listen and to reflect.

The power of the priests and monks has changed very much since the revolution. At Buenos Aires most of the convents have been suppressed, and the general wish of almost all parties is to suppress the remainder. Occasionally, an old mendicant friar is seen, dressed in grey sackcloth, and covered with dirt; but as he walks through the street, looking on the ground, his emaciated cheek and sunken eye show that his power is crushed, and his influence gone. The churches have lost their plate, the candles are yellow, the pictures are bad, and the images are dressed in coarse English cotton. On great days, the ladies of Buenos Aires, dressed in their best clothes, are seen going to church, followed by a black child, in yellow or green livery, who carries in his arms an English hearth-rug, always of the most brilliant colors, on which the lady kneels, with the black child behind her; but generally the churches are deserted, and nobody is to be seen in them but a decrepit old woman or two, whispering into the chinks of the confessional box. The sad consequence of all this is that at Buenos Aires there is very little religion at all. At Mendoza there are several people who wish to put down the priests; still, however, they have evidently considerable power.

Once a year the men and women are called upon to live for nine days in a sort of barrack, which, as a great favor, I was allowed to visit. It is filled with little cells, and the men and women, at different times, are literally shut up in these holes, to fast and whip themselves. I asked several people seriously whether this punishment was bona fide performed, and they assured me that most of them whipped themselves till they brought blood. One day, I was talking very earnestly to a person at Mendoza, at the hotel, when a poor-looking monk arrived with a little image surrounded with flowers: this image my friend was obliged to kiss, and the monk then took it to every individual in the hotel—to the landlord, his servants, and even to the black cook, who all kissed it, and then of course paid for the honor. The cook gave the monk two eggs.

The priests at Mendoza lead a dissolute life; most of them have families, and several live openly with their children. Their principal amusement, however, odd as it may sound, is cockfighting every Thursday and Sunday. I was riding one Sunday when I first discovered their arena, and got off my horse to look at it. It was crowded with priests, who had each a fighting cock under his arm; and it was surprising to see how earnest and yet how long they were in making their bets. I stayed there more than an hour, during which time the cocks were often upon the point of fighting, but the bet was not settled. Besides the priests, there were a number of little dirty boys, and one pretty-looking girl present. While they were arranging their bets, the boys began to play, so the judge instantly ordered all those who had no cocks to go out of the arena; upon which the poor girl and all the little boys were immediately turned out.

I soon got tired of the scene; but before I left them, I could not help thinking what an odd sight it was, and how justly shocked people in England would be to see a large body of clergymen fighting cocks upon a Sunday.

At San Juan the priests have rather more power than at Mendoza, and this they showed the other day, by taking the governor prisoner while in bed, and by burning, by the hands of the jailer, on the plaza, the Carta de Mayo, which, to encourage the settlement of the English in this province, had lately granted to strangers religious toleration. In the other provinces the priests have more or less power, according to their abilities, and generally according to their greater or less communication with Buenos Aires.

The religion of the gaucho is necessarily more simple than in the town, as his situation places him out of the reach of the priests. In almost all the huts there is a small image or picture, and the gauchos have sometimes a small cross round their necks. In order that their children should be baptized, they carry them on horseback to the nearest church, and I believe the dead are generally thrown across a horse and buried in consecrated ground: though the courier and postilion who were murdered, and whose funeral service I attended, were buried in the ruins of an old hut in the middle of the Plain of Santa Fe. When a marriage is contracted, the young gaucho takes his bride behind him on his horse, and in the course of a few days they can generally get to a church.

II

BUENOS AIRES

The town of Buenos Aires is far from being an agreeable residence for those who are accustomed to English comforts. The water is extremely impure, scarce, and consequently expensive. The town is badly paved and dirty, and the houses are the most comfortless abodes I ever entered. The walls, from the climate, are damp, mouldy, and discolored. The floors are badly paved with bricks, which are generally cracked, and often in holes. The roofs have no ceiling, and the families have no idea of warming themselves except by huddling round a fire of charcoal, which is put outside the door until the carbonic acid gas has rolled away.

Some of the principal families at Buenos Aires furnish their rooms in a very expensive, but comfortless manner: they put down upon the brick floor a brilliant Brussels carpet, hang a luster from the rafters, and place against the damp wall, which they whitewash, a number of tawdry North American chairs. They get an English pianoforte, and some marble vases, but they have no idea of grouping their furniture into a comfortable form: the ladies sit with their backs against the walls without any apparent means of employing themselves; and when a stranger calls upon them, he is much surprised to find that they have the uncourteous custom of never rising from their chairs. I had no time to enter into any society at Buenos Aires, and the rooms looked so comfortless, that, to tell the truth, I had little inclination. The society of Buenos Aires is composed of English and French merchants, with a German or two. The foreign merchants are generally the agents of European houses; and as the customs of the Spanish South Americans, their food, and the hours at which they eat it, are different from those of the

English and French, there does not appear to be much communication between them.

At Buenos Aires the men and women are rarely seen walking together; at the theater they are completely separated; and it is cheerless to see all the ladies sitting together in the boxes, while the men are in the pit—slaves, common sailors, soldiers, and merchants, all members of the same republic.

The town is furnished with provisions by the gauchos in a manner that shows a great want of attention to those arrangements which are generally met with in civilized communities. Milk, eggs, fruit, vegetables, and beef are brought into the town by individuals at a gallop, and they are only to be had when they choose to bring them. (One of the most striking pictures in and near Buenos Aires is the young gaucho who brings milk. The milk is carried in six or eight large earthen bottles, which hang on each side of the saddle. There is seldom room for the boy's legs, and he therefore generally turns his feet up behind him on the saddle, and sits like a frog. One meets these boys in squads of four or five, and the manner in which they gallop in their red cloth caps, with their scarlet ponchos flying behind them, is a singular appearance. The butchers' shops are covered carts, which are not very agreeable objects. The beef, mangled in a most shocking manner, is swinging about; and I have constantly seen a large piece tied by a strip of hide to the tail of the cart, and dragged along the ground, with a dog trying to tear it.)

The articles of life are brought together without due arrangement, and the consequence is, that (excepting beef) they are dearer than in London, and sometimes are not to be had at all. I happened to leave Buenos Aires just as the fig season was over, and though it was the middle of summer, no fruit was to be had: the townspeople seemed to be quite satisfied with this reason, and I could not persuade them that someone should arrange a constant supply and succession of fruits, and not leave it entirely to the gaucho. But the same want of arrangement exists in all instances. If one has been taken out to dinner in a carriage, and in the evening ventures to inquire why it has not arrived, the answer is that it is raining, and that those who let carriages will not allow them to go out if it rains.

During the short time I was at Buenos Aires, I lived in a house out of the town, which was opposite the English burying ground, and very near the place where the cattle were killed. This latter spot was about four or five acres, and was altogether devoid of pasture; at one end of it there was a large corral enclosed by rough stakes, and divided into a number of pens, each of which had a separate gate. These *cells* were always full of cattle doomed for slaughter. I several times had occasion to ride over this field, and it was curious to see its different appearances. In passing it in the day or evening, no human being was to be seen: the cattle up to their knees in mud, and with nothing to eat, were standing in the sun, occasionally lowing, or rather roaring to each other. The ground in every direction was covered with groups of large white gulls, some of which were earnestly pecking at the slops of blood which they had surrounded, while others were standing upon their tiptoes, and flapping their wings as if to recover their appetite. Each slop of blood was the spot where a bullock had died; it was all that was left of his history, and pigs and gulls were rapidly consuming it. Early in the morning no blood was to be seen; a number of horses, with the lassos hanging to their saddles, were standing in groups apparently asleep: the mataderos were either sitting or lying on the ground close to the stakes of the corral, and smoking cigars; while the cattle, without metaphor, were waiting until the last hour of their existence should strike; for as soon as the clock of the Recoleta struck, the men all vaulted on their horses, the gates of all the cells were opened, and in a very few seconds, there was a scene of apparent confusion which it is quite impossible to describe. Every man had a wild bullock at the end of his lasso; some of these animals were running away from the horses, and some were running at them; many were roaring, some were hamstrung, and running about on their stumps; some were killed and skinned, while occasionally one would break the lasso. The horse would often fall upon his rider, and the bullock endeavor to regain his liberty, until the horsemen at full speed caught him with the lasso, tripping him off the ground in a manner that might apparently break every bone in his body. I was more than once in the middle of this odd scene, and was really sometimes obliged to gallop for my life, without exactly knowing where to go, for it was often Scylla and Charybdis.

I was one day going home from this scene when I saw a man on foot select a very large pig from a herd, and throw a lasso over his neck; he pulled it with all his strength, but the pig had no idea of obeying the summons: in an instant a little child rode up, and very quietly taking the end of the lasso from the man, he lifted up the sheepskin which covered the saddle, fixed the lasso to the ring which is there made for it, and then instantly set off at gallop: never did any one see an obstinate animal so completely conquered! With his tail pointing to the ground, hanging back, and with his four feet all scratching along the ground like the teeth of a harrow, he followed the boy evidently altogether against his will; and the sight was so strange, that I instantly galloped after the pig, to watch his countenance. He was as obstinate as ever until the lasso choked him, and he then fainted, and fell on his side. The boy dragged him in this state, at a gallop, more than three-quarters of a mile over hard rough ground, and at last suddenly stopped, and jumping off his horse, began to unloose the lasso:—"Está muerto!" (he is dead), said I to the boy, really sorry for the pig's fate. "Está vivo!" exclaimed the child, as he vaulted on his horse, and galloped away. I watched the pig for some time, and was observing the blood on his nose, when, to my great surprise, he began to kick his hind leg: he then opened his mouth, and at last his eyes; and after he had looked about him, a little like Clarence after his dream, he got up, and very leisurely walked to a herd of ten or twelve pigs of about the same size as himself, who were about twenty yards off. I slowly followed him, and when I came to the herd, I saw they had every one of them bloody noses.

The house which I had near Buenos Aires was not only opposite the English burying ground, but on the road to the Recoleta, which was the great burying place for the town; about half-a-dozen funerals passed my window every day, and during the few days I was at Buenos Aires, I scarcely ever rode into the town without meeting one.

Although the manners, customs, amusements, and fashions of different nations are constantly changing, and are generally different in different climates, yet one would at first expect that so simple an act as that of consigning to its narrow bed the body of a dead man would, in all countries and in all places, be the same—but though death is the same, funerals are very different. In the old world, how often does the folly and vanity and vexation of spirit in which a man has lived accompany him to the tomb; and how often are the good feelings of the living overpowered by the vain pomp and ostentation which mocks the burial of the dead. In South America, the picture is a very different one, and certainly the way in which the people were buried at Buenos Aires appeared more strange to my eyes than any of the customs of the place. Of late years, a few of the principal people have been buried in coffins, but generally the dead are called for by a hack hearse, in which there is a fixed coffin, into which they are put, when away the man gallops with the corpse, and leaves it in the vestibule of the Recoleta. There is a small vehicle for children, which I really thought was a mountebank's cart; it was a light open tray, on wheels painted white, with light blue silk curtains, and driven at a gallop by a lad dressed in scarlet, with an enormous plume of white feathers in his hat. As I was riding home one day, I was overtaken by this cart (without its curtains, &c.) in which there was the corpse of a black boy nearly naked. I galloped along with it for some distance; the boy, from the rapid motion of the carriage, was dancing some-times on his back and sometimes on his face; occasionally his arm or leg would get through the bar of the tray, and two or three times I really thought the child would have been out of the tray altogether. The bodies of the rich were generally attended by their friends; but the carriages with four people in each were seldom able to go as fast as the hearse.

I went one day to the Recoleta, and just as I got there, the little hearse drove up to the gate. The man who had charge of the burial place received from the driver a ticket, which he read, and put into his pocket; the driver then got into the tray, and taking out a dead infant of about eight months old, he gave it to the man, who carried it, swinging by one of its arms, into the square-walled burial ground, and I followed him. He went to a spot about ten yards from the corner, and then, without putting his foot upon the spade, or at all lifting up the ground, he scratched a place not so deep as the furrow of a plough. While he was doing this, the poor little infant was lying before us on the ground on its back; it had one eye open, and the other shut; its face was unwashed, and a small piece of dirty cloth was tied round its middle: the man, as he was talking to me, placed the child in the little furrow, pushed its arms to its side with the spade, and covering it so barely with earth that part of the cloth was still visible, he walked away and left it. I took the spade, and was going to bury the poor child myself, when I recollected that as a stranger I should probably give offence, and I therefore walked towards the gate. I met the same man, with an assistant, carrying a tray, in which was the body of a very old man, followed by his son, who was about forty; the party were all quarrelling, and remained disputing for some minutes after they had brought the body to the edge of the trench. This trench was about seven feet broad, and had been dug from one wall of the burial ground to the other: the corpses were buried across it by fours, one above another, and there was a moveable shutter which went perpendicularly across the trench, and was moved a step forwards as soon as the fourth body was interred. One body had already been interred; the son jumped down upon it, and while he was thus in the grave, standing upon one body and leaning against three, the two gravediggers gave him his father, who was dressed in a long, coarse, white linen shirt. The grave was so narrow that the man had great difficulty in laying the body in it, but as soon as he had done so, he addressed the lifeless corpse of his father, and embraced it with a great deal of feeling: the situation of the father and son, although so very unusual, seemed at the moment anything but unnatural. In scrambling out of the grave, the man very nearly knocked a woman out of the tier of corpses at his back; and as soon as he was up, the two attendants with their spades threw earth down upon the face and the white dress of the old man, until both were covered with a very thin layer of earth: the two men then jumped down with heavy wooden rammers, and they really rammed the corpse in that sort of way that, had the man been alive, he would have been killed; and we then all walked away.

III

Modes of Travel

There are two ways of traveling across the pampas, in a carriage or on horseback. The carriages are without springs, either of wood or iron, but they are very ingeniously slung on hide ropes, which make them quite easy enough. There are two sorts of carriages, a long vehicle on four wheels, like a van (with a door behind), which is drawn by four or six horses, and which can carry eight people; and a smaller carriage on two wheels, of about half the length, which is usually drawn by three horses.

When I first went across the pampas, I purchased for my party a large carriage, and also an enormous, two-wheeled, covered cart, which carried about twenty-five hundred weight of miners' tools, &c. I engaged a capataz (headman), and he hired for me a number of peons, who were to receive thirty or forty dollars each for driving the vehicles to Mendoza.

The day before we started, the capataz came to me for some money to purchase hides, in order to prepare the carriages in the usual way. The hides were soaked, and then cut into long strips, about three-quarters of an inch broad, and the pole, as also almost all the woodwork of the carriage, were firmly bound with the wet hide, which, when dry, shrunk into a band almost as hard as iron. The spokes of the wheels, and, very much to our astonishment, the fellies or the circumference of the wheels were similarly bound, so that they actually traveled on the hide. We all declared it would be cut before it got over the pavement of Buenos Aires, but it went perfectly sound for seven hundred miles, and was then only cut by some sharp granite rocks over which we were obliged to drive.

With respect to provisions, we were told (truly

enough) that there is little to be had on the pampas but beef and water; and a quantity of provisions, with cherry brandy, &c., &c., was collected by the party, some of whom, I believe, fancied that I was going to take them, not to El Dorado, but to "that undiscovered country from which no traveler returns"; however, when we were ready to start, one of them found out that the loaves and fishes, the canteen, &c., were all left out (whether by accident or design, it matters not), and they then all cheerfully consented to "rough it," which is really the only way to travel without vexation in any country. We took some brandy and tea with us, but so destitute were we of other luxuries that the first day we had nothing to drink our tea out of but eggshells.

As it had been reported to the government of Buenos Aires that the Pampas Indians had invaded the country through which we had to pass, the minister was kind enough to give me an order to a commandant who was on the road with troops, for assistance if required; and besides this, we purchased a dozen muskets, some pistols, and sabers which were slung to the roof of the carriage.

As it is customary to pay the peons half their money in advance, and as men who have been paid in advance have in all countries a number of thirsty friends, it is very difficult to collect all the drivers. Ours were of all colors, black, white, and red; and they were as wild a looking crew as ever was assembled. We had six horses in the carriage, six in the cart, each of which was ridden by a peon, and I, with one of the party, rode.

The traveling across the pampas a distance of more than nine hundred miles is really a very astonishing effort. The country, as before described, is flat, with no road but a track, which is constantly changed. The huts, which are termed posts, are at different distances, but upon an average, about twenty miles from each other; and in traveling with carriages, it is necessary to send a man on before, to request the gauchos to collect their horses.

The manner in which the peons drive is quite extraordinary. The country, being in a complete state of nature, is intersected with streams, rivulets, and even rivers, with pantanos (marshes), &c., through which it is absolutely necessary to drive. In one instance the carriage, strange as it may seem, goes through a lake, which of course is not deep. The banks of the rivulets are often very precipitous, and I constantly remarked that we drove over and through places which in Europe any military officer would, I believe, without hesitation report as impassable.

The mode in which the horses are harnessed is admirably adapted to this sort of rough driving. They draw by the saddle instead of the collar, and having only one trace instead of two, they are able, on rough ground, to take advantage of every firm spot; where the ground will only once bear, every peon takes his own path, and the horses' limbs are all free and unconstrained.

In order to harness or unharness, the peons have only to hook and unhook the lasso which is fixed to their saddle; and this is so simple and easy that we constantly observed when the carriage stopped that before any one of us could jump out of it, the peons were unhooked, and were out of our sight to catch fresh horses in the corral.

In a gallop, if anything was dropped by one of the peons, he would unhook, gallop back, and overtake the carriage without its stopping for him. I often thought how admirably in practice this mode of driving would suit the particular duties of that noble branch of our army, the Horse Artillery.

The rate at which the horses travel (if there are enough of them) is quite surprising. Our cart, although laden with twenty-five hundred weight of tools, kept up with the carriage at a hand gallop. Very often, as the two vehicles were going at this pace, some of the peons, who were always in high spirits, would scream out, "Ah, mi patrón!" and then all shriek and gallop with the carriage after me; and very frequently I was unable to ride away from them.

But strange as the account of this sort of driving may

sound, the secret would be discovered by anyone who could see the horses arrive. In England, horses are never seen in such a state; the spurs, heels, and legs of the peons are literally bathed with blood, and from the sides of the horses the blood is constantly flowing rather than dropping.

After this description, in justice to myself, I must say, that it is impossible to prevent it. The horses cannot trot, and it is impossible to draw the line between cantering and galloping, or, in merely passing through the country, to alter the system of riding, which all over the pampas is cruel.

The peons are capital horsemen, and several times we saw them at a gallop throw the rein on the horse's neck, take from one pocket a bag of loose tobacco, and with a piece of paper, or a leaf of the Indian corn, make a cigar, and then take out a flint and steel and light it.

The post huts are from twelve to thirty-six miles, and in one instance fifty-four miles, from each other; and as it would be impossible to drag a carriage these distances at a gallop, relays of horses are sent on with the carriage, and are sometimes changed five times in a stage.

It is scarcely possible to conceive a wilder sight than our carriage and covered cart, as I often saw them, gallaping over the trackless plain, and preceded or followed by a troop of from thirty to seventy wild horses, all loose and galloping, driven by a gaucho and his son, and sometimes by a couple of children. (I was one day observing them, instead of looking before me, when my horse fell in a vizcachera, and rolled over upon my arm. It was so crushed that it made me very faint; but before I could get into my saddle, the carriages were almost out of sight, and while the sky was still looking green from the pain I was enduring, I was obliged to ride after them, and I believe I had seven miles to gallop as hard as my horse could go, before I could overtake the carriage to give up my horse.) The picture seems to correspond with the danger which positively exists in passing through uninhabited regions, which are so often invaded by the merciless Indians.

In riding across the pampas, it is generally the custom to take an attendant, and people often wait to accompany some carriage; or else, if they are in condition, ride with the courier, who gets to Mendoza in twelve or thirteen days. In case travelers wish to carry a bed and two small pormanteaus, they are placed upon one horse, which is either driven on before, or, by a halter, tied to the postilion's saddle.

The most independent way of traveling is without baggage, and without an attendant. In this case, the traveler starts from Buenos Aires or Mendoza with a postilion, who is changed at every post. He has to saddle his own horses, and to sleep at night upon the ground on his saddle; and as he is unable to carry any provisions, he must throw himself completely on the feeble resources of the country, and live on little else than beef and water.

It is of course a hard life; but it is so delightfully independent, and if one is in good riding condition, so rapid a mode of traveling that I twice chose it, and would always prefer it; but I recommend no one to attempt it, unless he is in good health and condition.

When I first crossed the pampas, I went with a carriage, and although I had been accustomed to riding all my life, I could not at all ride with the peons, and after galloping five or six hours was obliged to get into the carriage; but after I had been riding for three or four months, and had lived upon beef and water, I found myself in a condition which I can only describe by saying that I felt no exertion could kill me. Although I constantly arrived so completely exhausted that I could not speak, yet a few hours' sleep upon my saddle, on the ground, always so completely restored me that for a week I could daily be upon my horse before sunrise, could ride till two or three hours after sunset, and have really tired ten and twelve horses a day. This will explain the immense distances which people in South America are said to ride, which I am confident could only be done on beef and water.

At first, the constant galloping confuses the head, and I have often been so giddy when I dismounted that I could scarcely stand; but the system, by degrees, gets accustomed to it, and it then becomes the most delightful life which one can possibly enjoy. It is delightful from its variety, and from the natural mode of reflecting which it encourages—for, in the grey of the morning, while the air is still frosty and fresh, while the cattle are looking wild and scared, and while the whole face of nature has the appearance of youth and innocence, one indulges in those feelings and speculations in which, right or wrong, it is so agreeable to err; but the heat of the day, and the fatigue of the body, gradually bring the mind to reason; before the sun has set many opinions are corrected, and, as in the evening of life, one looks back with calm regret upon the past follies of the morning.

In riding across the pampas with a constant succession of gauchos, I often observed that the children and the old men rode quicker than the young men. The children have no judgment, but they are so light, and always in such high spirits, that they skim over the ground very quickly. The old grey-headed gaucho is a good horseman, with great judgment, and although his pace is not quite so rapid as the children's, yet, from being constant and uniform, he arrives at his goal nearly in the same time. In riding with the young men, I found that the pace was unavoidably influenced by their passions, and by the subject on which we happened to converse; and when we got to the post, I constantly found that, somehow or other, time had been lost.

In crossing the pampas it is absolutely necessary to be armed, as there are many robbers or salteadores, particularly in the desolate province of Santa Fe.

The object of these people is of course money, and I therefore always rode so badly dressed, and so well armed, that although I once passed through them with no one but a child as a postilion, they thought it not worth their while to attack me. I always carried two brace of detonating pistols in a belt, and a short detonating double-barreled gun in my hand. I made it a rule never to be an instant without my arms, and to cock both barrels of my gun whenever I met any gauchos.

With respect to the Indians, a person riding can use no precaution, but must just run the gauntlet, and take his chance, which, if calculated, is a good one.

If he fall in with them, he may be tortured and killed, but it is very improbable that he should happen to find them on the road; however, they are so cunning, and ride so quick, and the country is so uninhabited, that it is impossible to gain any information about them: besides this, the people are so alarmed, and there are so many constant reports concerning them, that it becomes useless to attend to any, and I believe it is just as safe to ride towards the spot at which one hears they are, as to turn back.

The greatest danger in riding alone across the pampas is the constant falls which the horses get in the holes of the vizcachas. I calculated that, upon an average, my horse fell with me in a gallop once in every three hundred miles; and although, from the ground being very soft, I was never seriously hurt, yet previous to starting one cannot help feeling what a forlorn situation it would be, to break a limb, or dislocate a joint, so many hundred miles from any sort of assistance.

IV

SAN LUIS

Fifth day (from Buenos Aires). We arrived an hour after sunset—fortified post—scrambling in the dark for the kitchen—cook unwilling—correo (the courier) gave us his dinner—huts of wild-looking people—three women and girls almost naked ("They be so wild as the donkey," said one of the Cornish party, smiling; he then very gravely added, "and there be one thing, sir, that I do observe, which is, that the farther we do go, the wilder things do get!")—their strange appearance as they cooked our fowls. Our hut—old man immovable—María or Mariquita's figure—little mongrel boy—three or four other persons. Roof supported in the center by a crooked pole—holes in roof and walls—walls of mud, cracked and rent—a water jug in the corner on a three-pronged stick. Floor, the earth—the eight hungry peons, by moonlight, standing with their knives in their hands over a sheep they were going to kill, and looking on their prey like relentless tigers.

In the morning, Morales and the peons standing by the fire—the blaze making the scene behind them dark and obscure—the horizon like the sea, except here and there the back of a cow to be seen—wagon and coach just discernible.

In the hut all our party occupied with the baggage—lighted by a candle crooked and thin. Scene of urging the patrón to get horses, and Mariquita to get milk—the patrón wakening the black boy.

Twelfth day.—Left the post hut with three changes of horses to get to San Luis, distant thirty-six miles—inquired the way of one of the gauchos who was drawing the carriage—he dismounted and traced it with his finger on

33

the road—we were to turn off, when about three leagues, at a dead horse which we should see. I then galloped on with one of my party, knowing that we were to see no habitation until we got to San Luis—we had three hours and a half of daylight. About halfway we began to think we had lost our path; however, we were sure to be wrong if we stopped to debate, and we therefore galloped on. Our horses got tired, and the sun was nearly setting without any appearance of houses, but as the lower edge touched the horizon, we discovered a hut, and riding up to it, we were informed by a little girl that we were near San Luis. We got to the post just as it was dark, and eagerly inquired of the wild group if there was an inn in the town. "No hay! señor; no hay!" We then inquired for beds. "No hay! señor; no hay!"—"Is there a café?" "No hay! señor," in exactly the same tone of voice. When we looked round us, we found nothing but bare walls and fleas. We happened (that day) to have English saddles, and we therefore began to ask again about beds. The woman told us we should have hers, and in a few moments she brought mattress and all rolled up, and laid it down on the floor; however, when I cast my eyes on the blanket, and above all the sheets, I begged in the most earnest manner that she would let me have something a little cleaner. "Son limpias," (they are clean) said the woman, taking up the sheet, and pointing to a little spot which looked whiter than the rest. There was no use in arguing the point, so I walked out of the hut, leaving the corner of the sheet in the woman's hand, and declaring that it was quite impossible to sleep there.

I went to the door of the maestro de posta (postmaster), and told him that I had ridden all day without eating; that I was very hungry, and begged to know what we could have: "Lo que quiera, señor, tenemos todo" (whatever you choose, we have everything).

I knew too well what "todo" meant, and he accordingly explained to me that he had "carne de vaca and gallinas" (beef and fowls). I ordered a fowl, and then went to my room. The sight of the bed again haunted me, and after looking at it for some time with every inclination to persuade myself that it was even bearable, but in vain, I resolved to go to the governor, deliver my letters, and see what I could do with him.

I procured a guide, who was to lead me in the dark to the governor's house. After walking some distance, "Aquí está," said the man. "What, is that it?" said I, pointing to a door at which some black naked children were standing.—No, it was the next house.

The governor was not at home, but I found his wife sitting on a bed, surrounded by ladies—requested to sit down, but hurried off to the coronel—he was not at home, said the young lady, who begged me to sit down. Went to the barracks—my reception—an ordenanza or soldier ordered to return with me to the post, to desire the postmaster to treat me with particular respect. The town of San Luis by moonlight—no houses to be seen, but garden walls of mud. Went to look after my dinner—found the girl who was to cook it sitting in the smoke with the peons. I saw a black iron pot on the fire in which I supposed was my fowl—I asked if the fowl was there? "No, señor, aquí está," said the girl, throwing an old blanket off her bare shoulders, and showing me the fowl alive in her lap. I was going to complain, and I fear to swear, but the smoke so got into my eyes and mouth that I could neither see nor speak. At last I asked for eggs, "No hay, señor." "Good heavens!" said I, "in the capital of San Luis is there not one single egg?" "Yes," she said, but it was too late, she would get me some mañana (tomorrow). She asked me if I liked cheese. "Oh, yes," said I, eagerly. She gave me an enormous cheese, and insisted on my taking the whole of it, but she had no bread.

I had hurt my right arm by my horse falling; however, I carried the cheese into my room, and then did not know where to put it. The floor was filthy—the bed was worse, and there was nothing else; so supporting it with my lame arm, I stood for some seconds moralizing on the state of the capital of the province of San Luis.

V

The Gold Mines and Lavaderos
of La Carolina

Started at daybreak from San Luis, to go to the gold
mines and lavaderos (alluvial soil which is washed for
gold) of La Carolina, which are in the mountains on the
north of the town.

Drove a set of loose horses before us, and, about
twelve o'clock, stopped to change.

The horses were driven to the edge of a precipice
which was quite perpendicular, and which overhung a
torrent, and we formed a semicircle about them while the
peons began to catch them with the lasso, which they were
much afraid of. The horses were so crowded and scared
that I expected they would all have been over the precipice: at last the hind legs of one horse went down the cliff,
and he hung in a most extraordinary manner by the forelegs, with his nose resting on the ground, as far from him
as possible, to preserve his balance. As soon as we saw him
in this situation, we allowed the other horses to escape,
and in a moment the peon threw his lasso with the most
surprising precision, and it went below the animal's tail
like the breeching of harness. We then all hauled upon it,
and at last lifted the horse, and succeeded in dragging him
up; during the whole time he remained quiet, and to all
appearance perfectly conscious that the slightest struggle
would have been fatal to him. We then mounted our fresh
horses, and although the path over the mountains was so
steep and rugged that we were occasionally obliged to
jump a foot or two from one level to another, we scrambled
along with the loose horses before us, at the rate of nine or
ten miles an hour.

In the evening, we came to a small stream of water,
which led us to the wretched hamlet of La Carolina, which
is close to the mine.

A man offered us a shed to sleep in, which we readily accepted, and we then went into several of the huts, and conversed with the poor people, who had heard of rich English associations, and who thought we were come to give them everything they could desire.

In the evening we got some supper, and slept on the ground in an outhouse. We had observed a very savage dog tied up in the yard, which was constantly trying to get at us. In the middle of the night, while the moon was shining upon us through some holes in the roof, this dog walked in, and after smelling us all, he went to sleep among us.

The whole of the next day we spent in the mines and the lavaderos, and in the evening I walked alone into a little garden, and looked among the soil for gold. I really was able to find a very few particles, and it was singular to collect such a commodity in the gardens of such very poor people.

On my return I called at several of the huts, to receive some gold dust which I had promised to purchase of them. It happened that I had nothing but a quantity of four-dollar gold pieces, and although they were current all over South America, I found, to my very great astonishment, that no one here would take them. In vain I assured them of their value, but these poor people (accustomed to change gold for silver) all shook their fingers in my face, and in different voices exclaimed "No vale nada," (gold is worth nothing), and among such wild mountains, the great moral truth of their assertion rushed very forcibly into my mind.

I offered them the piece of four dollars for what they only asked two and three dollars, but they would not take it; and we had hardly silver enough among us to remunerate our landlord for the board and lodging which he had afforded us.

Our horses which we had brought from San Luis were caught, and put into the corral the evening before we left the town, and they had consequently nothing to eat all that night.

The following day, as I have stated, we rode them sixty miles, and as it was then too late to turn them out, they were kept by the peon in the yard all that night.

The next day, while we were inspecting the mines, they were turned out for four or five hours to graze among stones and rocks, where there was apparently nothing for them to eat, and they were then brought into the yard, where they remained fasting all night. The next morning before daybreak we mounted them, and rode sixty miles back to San Luis, and as some of the party came in very late, I rather believe that the postmaster kept them in his corral all night, and that the following morning they were driven to the plain.

The poor creatures must of course have suffered very much, but I did not know that at Carolina there would have been nothing for them to eat; and when we were there, I believe it was merciful to them not to stay; but the truth is that the business I was on was of such importance that I really had not time to think about it.

VI

MENDOZA

The town of Mendoza is situated at the foot of the Andes, and the country around it is irrigated by cuts from the Río Mendoza. This river bounds the west side of the town, and from it, on the east side, there is a cut or canal about six feet wide, containing nearly as much water as would turn a large mill. This stream supplies the town with water, and at the same time adorns and refreshes the alameda or public walk. It waters the streets which descend from it to the river, and can also be conducted into those which are at right angles.

Mendoza is a neat small town, built upon the usual plan. The streets are all at right angles; there is a plaza or square, on one side of which is a large church, and several other churches and convents are scattered over the town. The houses are only one story high, and all the principal ones have a porte cochère, which enters a small court, round the four sides of which the house extends.

The houses are built of mud, and are roofed with the same. The walls are whitewashed, which gives them a neat appearance, but the insides of the houses, until they are whitewashed, look like an English barn. The walls are of course very soft; occasionally a large piece of them comes off, and they are of that consistency that, in a very few moments, a person, either with a spade or a pickaxe, could cut his way through any wall in the town. Several of the principal houses have glass in the window sashes, but the greatest number have not. The houses are almost all little shops, and the goods displayed are principally English cottons.

The inhabitants are apparently a very quiet, respectable set of people. The governor, who is an old man, has the manners and the appearance of a gentleman: he has a large family of daughters, who are pleasing-looking girls. The men are dressed in blue or white jackets, without skirts. The women are only seen in the day sitting at their windows, in complete dishabille, but in the evening they come upon the alameda, dressed with a great deal of taste, in evening dresses and low gowns, and completely in the costume of London or Paris. The manner in which all the people seem to associate together, shows a great deal of good feeling and fellowship, and I certainly never saw less apparent jealousy in any place.

The people, however, are extremely indolent. A little after eleven o'clock in the morning, the shopkeepers make preparations for the siesta; they begin to yawn a little, and slowly to put back the articles which they have, during the morning, displayed on their tables. About a quarter before twelve they shut up the shops, the window shutters throughout the town are closed, or nearly so, and no individual is to be seen until five, and sometimes until six o'clock, in the evening.

During this time I used generally to walk about the town to make a few observations. It was really singular to stand at the corner of the right-angled streets, and in every direction to find such perfect solitude in the middle of the capital of a province. The noise occasioned by walking was like the echo which is heard in pacing by oneself up the long aisle of a church or cathedral, and the scene resembled the deserted streets of Pompeii.

In passing some of the houses I often heard people snoring, and when the siesta was over, I was often much amused at seeing the people awaken, for there is infinitely more truth and pleasure in thus looking behind the scenes of private life, than in making formal observations on man when dressed and prepared for his public performance. The people generally lie on the ground or floor of the room, and the group is often amusing.

I saw one day an old man (who was one of the principal people in the town) fast asleep and happy. The old woman his wife was awake, and was sitting up in easy dishabille scratching herself, while her daughter, who was a very pretty-looking girl of about seventeen, was also awake, but was lying on her side kissing a cat.

In the evening the scene begins to revive. The shops are opened; a number of loads of grass are seen walking about the streets, for the horse that is carrying them is completely hid. Behind the load a boy stands on the extremity of the back; and to mount and dismount he climbs up by the animal's tail. A few gauchos are riding about, selling fruit; and a beggar on horseback is occasionally seen, with his hat in his hand, singing a psalm in a melancholy tone.

As soon as the sun has set, the alameda is crowded with people, and the scene is very singular and interesting. The men are sitting at tables, either smoking cigars or eating ices; the ladies are sitting on the mud benches which are on both sides of the alameda. This alameda is a walk nearly a mile long, between two rows of tall poplars; on one side of it are the garden walls of the town, concealed by roses and shrubs, and on the other the stream of water which supplies the town.

It will hardly be credited that, while this alameda is filled with people, women of all ages, without clothes of any sort or kind, are bathing in great numbers in the stream which literally bounds the promenade. Shakespeare tells us, that "the chariest maid is prodigal enough if she unveil her beauties to the moon," but the ladies of Mendoza, not contented with this, appear even before the sun; and in the mornings and evenings they really bathe without any clothes in the Río Mendoza, the water of which is seldom up to their knees, the men and women all together; and certainly, of all the scenes which in my life I have witnessed, I never beheld one so indescribable.

However, to return to the alameda—the walk is often illuminated in a very simple manner by paper lamps, which are cut into the shapes of stars, and are lighted by a single candle. There is generally a band of music playing, and at the end of the walk is a temple built of mud, which is very elegant in its form, and of which it may truly be said "materiam superabat opus."

The few evenings I was at Mendoza, I always went as a complete stranger to this alameda to eat ices, which, after the heat of the day, were exceedingly delightful and refreshing; and as I put spoonful after spoonful into my mouth, looking above me at the dark outline of the cordillera, and listening to the thunder which I could sometimes hear rumbling along the bottoms of the ravines, and sometimes resounding from the tops of the mountains, I used always to acknowledge that if a man could but bear an indolent life, there can be no spot on earth where he might be more indolent and more independent than at Mendoza, for he might sleep all day, and eat ices in the evening, until his hourglass was out. Provisions are cheap, and the people who bring them quiet and civil; the climate is exhausting, and the whole population indolent—"Mais que voulez-vous?" how can the people of Mendoza be otherwise? Their situation dooms them to inactivity— they are bounded by the Andes and by the pampas, and, with such formidable and relentless barriers around them, what have they to do with the history, or the improvements, or the notions of the rest of the world? Their wants are few, and nature readily supplies them—the day is long, and therefore as soon as they have had their breakfasts, and have made a few arrangements for their supper, it is so very hot that they go to sleep, and what else could they do better?

VII

Across the Pampas

Returned to the fonda in the evening at ten o'clock, and found the two horses standing in the yard with nothing to eat, and a young gaucho, who was to accompany me as postilion, lying on the ground asleep on his saddle. Next morning before daybreak, got up, saddled my horse, and with my saddle as my bed, and some pistols and money, commenced my gallop for Buenos Aires.

Country to be described—delightful feeling of independence at the mode of traveling—air frosty, and ground hard. The sun rose, and shortly after got to the first post. Had a letter for the lady from her husband who was at Mendoza—went to give it to her, while the gaucho who was to accompany me was driving the horses into the corral—found the lady in bed. "Siéntese, señor," said she, pointing to an old chair which was at the head of the bed —sat down, and told her the letter was from her husband —she placed it under her pillow, and then offered me some maté, but I had no time to wait for it, and started.

At third post from Mendoza, the postmaster, who might be exhibited in England as a curious specimen of an indolent man, to everything I said, replied "*st*"—it was but an aspiration, and he seemed never to have said any other word—I had twice passed his house, and it was always the same *st !*

Galloped on with no stopping, but merely to change horses until five o'clock in the evening—very tired indeed, but on coming to the post hut, saw the horses in the corral, and resolved to push on. Started with a fresh horse, and a young gaucho, who, singing as he went, galloped like the wind; the sun set, and it got so dark that, for more than an hour, I expected that every moment the boy would get away from me, as the road was rough, and through wood.

At half-past seven, after having galloped a hundred and fifty-three miles, and been fourteen hours and a half on horseback, got to the post—found the hut occupied by some people who had arrived in a carriage—quite exhausted—nothing to eat—asked for bread, they had none—I really could scarcely speak—carried my saddle into a shed—two children asleep, and one black girl—lay down upon the ground, and instantly fell asleep—was awakened in two or three hours by the woman of the post, who had brought me some soup with meat in it—ate it all up, and again dropped off to sleep—an hour before daylight was awakened by the gaucho who was to go with me. "Vamos, señor!" said he, in a sharp, impatient tone of voice—got up, had some maté, mounted my horse, and as I galloped along felt pleased that the sun which had left me the evening before thirty miles nearer Mendoza, should find me at my work. At first post detained fifteen minutes for horses—the stage the longest between Mendoza and Buenos Aires, being fifty-one miles—the woman would only give me one spare horse, which we drove before us. Galloped my horse till he came to a standstill, and then got on the fresh one, and left the postilion behind. In about an hour this other horse quite done up—by constant spurring could just keep him in a canter—at last down he fell, and my foot hung in the stirrup—my long spur was also entangled in the sheepskin which was above my saddle—saw by the panting of the horse's flank and nostrils that he was too tired to be off with me. Mounted and cantered him till he fell down on my other leg, and I was then lame on both legs—overtook a boy driving some loose horses—took one of them, and my horse was driven among the flock, until we came to the post. Postmaster very kind, and ordered a gaucho to give me an easy-going horse, as both my legs hurt me very much—started with a boy, but our horses were done up before we got to San Luis—obliged to walk part of the distance, and then by kicking and spurring got into San Luis just as the sun set.

At San Luis was advised by groups of people, not to

go on by myself, as the courier and postilion (from Buenos Aires), with their horses and a dog, had just been found on the road with their throats cut—advised to join the courier who was just setting out for Buenos Aires. Accordingly, next morning started with the courier and three peons as guards, all armed with old pistols and guns. Courier a little old man of about fifty-five years of age— had been riding all his life—had a face like a withered apple—carried his pistol in his hand—told me he was father to the courier who had just been murdered—that he was his only son—that he had just succeeded in getting him the appointment—that he was nineteen—and that it was his first journey as courier—that he had no pistols, not even a knife—that it was barbarous to kill him—that he must have died like a lamb, &c. &c. This story he repeated at every post hut, and people were so fond of asking for it, and he so willing to give it, that we lost many minutes at each post. He would relate it to anybody—at one post he told it to a great rough mongrel-looking fellow, who was sitting on a stone while a little girl was combing his woolly hair—"*¿'En dos?*" said the little girl who had divided his hair at the back of his head, and who proposed to plait it into two tails—"Sí!" grunted her father, half-asleep, and nodding his head, as he listened to the courier's story. We therefore rode all day, and only went a hundred and two miles. Next morning off before sunrise, and took a postilion, and traveling by myself got on much quicker, but the horses still weak, and in the whole day could only proceed a hundred and ten miles.

Two more days rode from morning till night, sleeping on the ground, with nothing to eat but beef—at last came to that part of the province of Santa Fe near which the courier had been murdered. The postmaster refused to give me horses to go on unless I could find a guard, as he said the postilions would not go by themselves; he insisted on my waiting for the courier, and I accordingly lost half a day, as he did not arrive till night. Next morning at daybreak got up—saw the poor old courier lying on his saddle

—he had a cigar in his mouth, and for a long time he remained on his back praying and crossing himself. Started with the master of the post, an additional gaucho, and the postilion, all armed—very little conversation. As we approached the spot, it appeared as if they all expected that the salteadores would be there—after riding some leagues, left the road, and galloped through the dry grass towards a small black-looking hut in ruins. It was one of those which had been burnt by the Indians, and the whole family had been murdered in it. When we got to it, I looked around me, and no other hut or habitation was to be seen; there were no cattle, and when a few gamas (deer), which for a few moments were in sight, had fled away, we were left completely to ourselves, and not a bird or any animal was to be seen. We were in the center of a deserted province. We galloped up to the hut—it was built of large unbaked bricks and mud; the roof had been burnt—one of the gables had fallen to half its height—the other looked nearly falling—one wall had fallen, and we all rode up to this side of the hut. Close to us there was a deep well, into which the salteadores had thrown all the bodies—first the courier and postilion, then the dog, and then the horses. The carcasses of the horses lay before us— they were nearly eaten up by the eagles and vizcachas. The dog had not been touched—he was a very large one —and from the heat of the weather he was now bloated up to a size quite extraordinary—his throat was cut, and in my life I never saw so much expression in the countenance of a dead animal—his lip was curled up, and one could not but fancy that it expressed the feelings of rage and fidelity under which he had evidently fought to the last. In the hut lay the bodies of the courier and postilion with their throats cut (they had been taken out of the well by some gauchos)—they were barely covered over with some of the loose bricks from the wall. Some pieces of the courier's poncho were lying about, as also several of the covers of the letters which the murderers had opened. In the center of the hut were the white ashes of a fire which they had kindled—at the corner of the hut stood a solitary peach tree in blossom—its contrast with the scene before us was very striking. The old courier said something to the postmaster, who immediately climbed upon the ruined wall, and threw down some loose bricks—he fell—burst of laughter—we all got off our horses, and we covered the bodies over with bricks—"Con que, señores," said the old man, "haremos una oración para el difunto"—we all took off our hats, and stood round the pile—opposite were our horses looking at us—the old man had thrown the handkerchief off his head, and his beard, which was of four-days growth, was quite white—he stood over the body of his only son, and offered up some prayer, to which all the gauchos joined their responses. I joined and crossed myself with them, for as the courier looked at me, I was anxious to assist in alleviating the sorrows of an old man, and entertaining my own feelings, which it is not necessary to describe.

As soon as the ceremony was over (it lasted about two minutes) we put on our hats. "Con que, señores," said the old man; and after a long pause, "vamos!" said he, upon which the party split into groups to light cigars. I had scarcely lighted mine, when the old man came up to light his. His son's body was at our feet, but he put his face close to mine, and as he was sucking and blowing, with that earnestness of countenance which is only known to those who are in the habit of lighting a cigar, I could not help thinking what an odd scene was before me. However, we mounted our horses—I took a last farewell look at the peach tree, and we then all galloped across the dry brown grass, to regain the road, and the few minutes of time which we had thus spent at the hut.

We galloped on till sunset, when we came to a post hut, from which a party of five or six gauchos were just starting to go to the next hut, which was twenty-four miles; and as I was anxious to get on, I accompanied them.

There was but little twilight—no moon—the sky soon

became black, and in less than half an hour it was so dark, that I can declare I could not see my hand before me. The gauchos, who had been drinking pretty freely, kept together, and galloped on in line, talking and laughing very loudly: occasionally one of them gave a shrill, sudden whistle—a signal that his horse had just passed a vizcachera; but the conversation never stopped, and they were apparently as much at their ease as if they had been riding in broad daylight.

My feelings, however, were very different; and it is almost impossible to describe the reluctance I felt to use my spurs, and the inclination I had to pull at my bridle; indeed it was as much as I could do to loosen my rein and gallop with them, or rather a few paces in their rear, for, to avoid vizcacheras, I thought it safest to follow their footsteps.

Had I known it would have been so dark, or that the gauchos would have gone at such a pace, I certainly would not have accompanied them; but having once started, I had no alternative; for as they would not stop for me, I felt that unless I kept close to them, I should lose myself, and should not know in what direction to ride; and also, as I expected every moment that my horse would tumble into the vizcacheras, I thought it better to fall in reach of assistance, than to make the *pas seul*. However, the danger after all is not what a stranger conceives it; and after a couple of hours' fear and uneasiness, I heard the dogs of the post hut barking before us; and riding up to the glimmering light, we each unsaddled our horses, and leaving them to go wherever they chose, we roasted some beef upon the embers.

I slept very soundly on my saddle, and started the next morning, with a little gaucho, before sunrise.

At some distance I saw a boy riding through the thistles and clover, and as he was swinging horizontally above his head the bolas or balls, I perceived he was hunting for ostriches, and I therefore rode up to him.

He was a black boy of about fourteen years of age,

slight, and well-made, but with scarcely anything on except the remains of a scarlet poncho. I asked him several questions—where he expected to find the ostriches, &c. &c. &c., to which he gave me no answer, but continued swinging the balls round his head, and looking about him. I was asking him some other insignificant questions when he cut me short, by asking me if I would sell my spurs; and before I had time to reply, an ostrich was in sight, and he darted away from me like an arrow. I was, just at the moment, among a group of vizcacheras—my horse fell, and before I had got clear of them, the boy was on the horizon, and from the contempt with which he had left me, I did not feel inclined to follow him.

The vizcacha is found all over the plains of the pampas. Like rabbits, they live in holes which are in groups in every direction, and which make galloping over these plains very dangerous. The manner, however, in which the horses recover themselves, when the ground over these subterranean galleries gives way, is quite extraordinary. In galloping after the ostriches, my horse has constantly broken in, sometimes with a hind leg, and sometimes with a fore one; he has even come down on his nose, and yet recovered; however, the gauchos occasionally meet with very serious accidents. I have often wondered how the wild horses could gallop about as they do in the dark, but I really believe they avoid the holes by smelling them, for in riding across the country, when it has been so dark that I positively could not see my horse's ears, I have constantly felt him, in his gallop, start a foot or two to the right or left, as if he had trod upon a serpent, which, I conceive, was to avoid one of these holes. Yet the horses do very often fall, and certainly, in the few months I was in the pampas, I got more falls than I ever before had, though in the habit of riding all my life. The gauchos are occasionally killed by these vizcacheras, and often break a limb.

In the middle of the pampas I once found a gaucho standing at the hut, with his left hand resting on the palm of his other hand, and apparently suffering great pain. He told me his horse had just fallen with him in a vizcachera, and he begged me to look at his hand. The large muscle of the thumb was very much-swelled, and every time I touched it with my forefinger, the poor fellow opened his mouth, and lifted up one of his legs. Being quite puzzled with one side of his hand, I thought I would turn it round, and look at the other side, and upon doing so, it was instantly evident that the thumb was out of joint. I asked him if there was any doctor near; the gaucho said he believed there was one at Córdoba, but as it was five hundred miles off, he might as well have pointed to the moon. "Is there no person," said I, "nearer than Córdoba, that understands anything about it?" "No hay, señor," said the poor fellow. I asked him what he intended to do with his thumb: he replied that he had washed it with salt and water, and then he earnestly asked me if that was good for it? "Sí! sí! sí!" said I, walking away in despair, for I thought it was useless to hint to him, that "not all the water in the wide rude sea" would put his thumb into its joint; and although I knew it ought to be pulled, yet one is so ignorant of such operations, that not knowing in what direction, I therefore left the poor fellow looking at his thumb, in the same attitude in which I found him. But, to return to the vizcachas.

These animals are never to be seen in the day, but as soon as the lower limb of the sun reaches the horizon, they are seen issuing from their holes in all directions, which are scattered in groups like little villages all over the pampas. The vizcachas, when full grown, are nearly as large as badgers; but their head resembles a rabbit, excepting that they have very large bushy whiskers.

In the evening they sit outside their holes, and they all appear to be moralizing. They are the most serious-looking animals I ever saw, and even the young ones are grey-headed, have mustachios, and look thoughtful and grave.

In the daytime their holes are always guarded by two

little owls, who are never an instant away from their posts. As one gallops by these owls, they always stand looking at the stranger, and then at each other, moving their old-fashioned heads in a manner which is quite ridiculous, until one rushes by them, when fear gets the better of their dignified looks, and they both run into the vizcacha's hole.

PROVINCE OF SANTA FE

Traveling from Buenos Aires to Mendoza by myself, with a birloche, or two-wheeled carriage—entrance behind— two side seats—had two peons—Pizarro, who had already traveled twelve hundred miles, and Cruz, a friend of Pizarro, had traveled for three days a hundred and twenty miles a day—Pizarro's fidelity and attention—at night when he got in, his dark black face tired, and covered with dust and perspiration—his tongue looked dry, and his whole countenance jaded—yet his frame was hard as iron. His first object at night to get me something to eat—to send out for a live sheep. He made a fire and cooked my supper—as soon as I had supped, he brought me a candle at the carriage door, and watched me while I undressed to sleep there—then wished me good night, got his own supper, and slept on his saddle at the wheel of the carriage. As soon as I awoke, and, before daylight, anxious to get on, I used to call out "Pizarro!" "Aquí está l'agua, señor," said he, in a patient low tone of voice—he knew I liked to have water to wash in the morning, and he used to get it for me, sometimes in a saucer, sometimes literally in a little maté cup, which did not hold more than an eggshell, and in spite of his fatigue he was always up before I awoke, and waiting at the door of the carriage till I should call for him.

Province of Santa Fe to be described—its wild, desolate appearance—has been so constantly ravaged by the Pampas Indians, that there are now no cattle in the whole province, and people are afraid to live there. On the right and left of the road, and distant thirty and forty miles, one occasionally sees the remains of a little hut which has been burnt by the Indians, and as one gallops along, the gaucho relates how many people were murdered in each—how many infants slaughtered—and whether the women were killed or carried away. The old post huts are also burnt—new ones have been built by the side of the ruins, but the rough plan of their construction shows the insecurity of their tenure. These huts are occupied only by men, who are themselves generally robbers, but in a few instances their families are living with them. When one thinks of the dreadful fate which has befallen so many poor families in this province, and that any moment may bring the Indians again among them, it is really shocking to see women living in such a dreadful situation—to fancy that they should be so blind, and so heedless of experience;—and it is distressing to see a number of innocent little children playing about the door of a hut, in which they may be all massacred, unconscious of the fate that may await them, or of the blood-thirsty, vindictive passions of man.

We were in the center of this dreary country—I always rode for a few stages in the morning, and I was with a young gaucho of about fifteen years of age, who had been born in the province—his father and mother had been murdered by the Indians—he had been saved by a man who had galloped away with him, but he was then an infant, and remembered nothing of it. We passed the ruins of a hut which he said had belonged to his aunt. He said that, about two years ago, he was at that hut with his aunt and three of his cousins, who were young men—that while they were conversing together a boy galloped by from the other post, and in passing the door screamed out, "los indios! los indios!"—that he ran to the door, and saw them galloping towards the hut without hats, all naked, armed with long lances, striking their mouths with their bridle hands, and uttering a shriek, which he described as making the earth tremble. He said that there were two horses outside the hut, bridled, but not saddled—that he leapt upon the back of one and galloped away—that one of the young men jumped on the other, and followed him about twenty yards, but that then he said something about his mother, and rode back to the hut—that just as he got there the Indians surrounded the hut, and that the last time he saw his cousins they were standing at the door with their knives in their hands—that several of the Indians galloped after him, and followed him more than a mile, but that he was upon a horse which was "muy ligero (very swift), muy ligero," said the boy; and as we galloped along he loosened his rein, and darting on before me, smiled at showing me the manner in which he escaped, and then curbing his horse to a hand gallop, continued his history.

He said that when the Indians found he was getting away from them, they turned back—that he escaped, and that when the Indians had left the province, which was two days after, he returned to the hut. He found it burnt, and saw his aunt's tongue sticking on one of the stakes of the corral; her body was in the hut; one of her feet was cut off at the ankle, and she had apparently bled to death. The three sons were outside the door naked, their bodies were covered with wounds, and their arms were gashed to the bone, by a series of cuts about an inch from each other, from the shoulder to the wrist.

The boy then left me at the next post, and I got into the carriage—the day getting hot, and the stage twenty-four miles. After galloping about an hour, I saw a large cloud of smoke on the horizon before me; and as the Indians often burn the grass when they enter the country, I asked Pizarro what it was? He replied, "Quién sabe, señor, what it may be"; however, on we galloped.

I took little notice of it, and began to think of the dreadful story the boy had told me, and of many similar ones which I had heard; for I had always endeavored to get at the history of the huts which were burnt, although I always found that the gauchos thought very little about it; and that the story was sometimes altogether in oblivion, before time had crumbled into dust the tottering mud walls which were the monuments of such dreadful cruelties.

It appears that the Pampas Indians, who, in spite of their ferocity, are a very brave and handsome race of men, occasionally invade "los cristianos," as the gauchos always term themselves, for two objects—to steal cattle, and for the pleasure of murdering the people; and that they will even leave the cattle to massacre their enemies.

In invading the country, they generally ride all night, and hide themselves on the ground during the day; or, if they do travel, crouch almost under the bellies of their horses, who by this means appear to be dismounted and at liberty. They usually approach the huts at night at a full gallop, with their usual shriek, striking their mouths with their hands—and this cry, which is to intimidate their enemies, is continued through the whole of the dreadful operation.

Their first act is to set fire to the roof of the hut and it is almost too dreadful to fancy what the feelings of a family must be, when, after having been alarmed by the barking of the dogs, which the gauchos always keep in great numbers, they first hear the wild cry which announces their doom, and in an instant afterwards find that the roof is burning over their heads.

As soon as the family rush out, which they of course are obliged to do, the men are wounded by the Indians with their lances, which are eighteen feet long, and as soon as they fall they are stripped of their clothes; for the Indians, who are very desirous to get the clothes of the Christians, are careful not to have them spoiled by blood. While some torture the men, others attack the children, and will literally run the infants through the body with their lances, and raise them to die in the air. The women are also attacked, and it would form a true but a dreadful picture to describe their fate, as it is decided by the momentary gleam which the burning roof throws upon their countenances.

The old women, and the ugly young ones, are instantly butchered; but the young and beautiful are idols, by whom even the merciless hand of the savage is arrested. Whether the poor girls can ride or not, they are instantly placed upon horses, and when the hasty plunder of the hut is concluded, they are driven away from its smoking ruins, and from the horrid scene which surrounds it.

At a pace which in Europe is unknown, they gallop over the trackless regions before them, fed upon mare's flesh, sleeping on the ground, until they arrive in the Indians' territory, when they have instantly to adopt the wild life of their captors.

I was informed by a very intelligent French officer, who was of high rank in the Peruvian army, that, on friendly terms, he had once passed through part of the territory of these Pampas Indians, in order to attack a tribe who were at war with them, and that he had met several of the young women who had been thus carried off by the Indians.

He told me that he had offered to obtain permission for them to return to their country, and that he had, in addition, offered them large sums of money if they would, in the meanwhile, act as interpreters; but they all replied that no inducement in the world should ever make them leave their husbands, or their children, and that they were quite delighted with the life they led.

While I was sitting upon the side seat of the carriage, reflecting on the cruelties which had been exercised in a country which, in spite of its history, was really wild and beautiful, and which possessed an air of unrestrained freedom which is always exhilarating, I remarked that the carriage was only at a walk, an occurrence which in South America had never before happened to me, and in an instant it stopped. "Vea, señor," said Pizarro, with a firm countenance, as he turned back to speak to me, "qué tanta gente!" he pointed with his right hand before him, and I saw that the smoke which I had before observed was dust, and in it I indistinctly saw a crowd of men on horseback in a sort of wild military array; and on both flanks, at a great distance off, individual horsemen, who were evidently on the lookout to prevent a surprise. Our horses were completely tired; the whole body were coming rapidly towards us, and to mend the matter, Pizarro told me that he was afraid they were los indios. "Señor," said he, with great coolness, and yet with a look of despair, "¿Tiene armas a fuego?" I told him I had none to spare, for I had only a short double-barreled gun and two brace of pistols. "Aquí un sable, Pizarro!" said I, pushing the handle of a saber towards him from the window of the carriage. "¡Qué sable!" said he, almost angrily; and raising his right arm perpendicularly over his head, in a sort of despair, he added, "contra tanta gente!" but while his arm was in the position described, "¡Vamos!" said he, in a tone of determined courage, and giving his hand half a turn, he spurred his jaded horse, and advanced instantly at a walk. Poor Cruz, the other peon, seemed to view the subject altogether in a different light; he said not a word, but as I cast a glance at him, I perceived that his horse, far from pulling the carriage, was now and then hanging back a little—a just picture of his rider's feelings. I could not help for a moment admiring Pizarro's figure, as I saw him occasionally digging his spurs into the side of his horse, which had me, the carriage, Cruz, and his horse to draw along; however, I now began to think of my own situation.

I earnestly wished I had never come into the country, and thought how unsatisfactory it was to be tortured and killed by mistake in other people's quarrels—however, this would not do. I looked towards the cloud of dust, and it was evidently much nearer. In despair, I got my gun and pistols, which were all loaded, and when I had disposed of them, I opened a small canvas bag which contained all my ammunition gimcracks, for my gun and pistols had all fulminating locks. I ranged all on the seat before me—the small powder flask, the buckshot, the bullets, the copper caps, and the punched cards; but the motion of the carriage danced them all together, and once or twice I felt inclined, in despair, to knock them all off the seat, for against so many people resistance was useless; however, on the other hand, mercy was hopeless, so I, at last, was driven to make the best of a very bad bargain.

The carriage, which had a window at each of the four sides, had wooden blinds, which moved horizontally. I therefore shut them all, leaving an embrasure of about two inches, and then for some seconds I sat looking at the crowd which was coming towards us.

As they came close to us, for until then I could scarcely see them for dust, I perceived that they had no spears, and next that they wore clothes; but as they had no uniforms I conceived that they were a crowd of montoneros, who are quite as cruel as the Indians; however, as soon as they came to us, and when some of them had passed us, Pizarro pulled up and talked to them. They were a body of seven hundred wild gauchos, collected and sent by the governors of Córdoba and some other provinces, to proceed to Buenos Aires to join the army against the Brazilians; and on their flank they had scouts, to prevent a surprise by the Indians, who had invaded the country only a few weeks before.

It was really a reprieve; everything I saw for the rest of the day pleased me—and for many days afterwards, I felt that I was enjoying a new lease of my life.

Two days afterwards, I was riding near the carriage, which was galloping along—Pizarro and Cruz looking fatigued and dirty, while the postilion before them, fresh and careless, was singing a Spanish song, when Pizarro's horse fell, and although Cruz tried to pull up, the postilion's horse dragged Pizarro along the ground at least twenty yards.

I really thought he was killed; however, he quietly declared he was not hurt, and, without saying one other word, he adjusted his saddle, and galloped on to the next stage. As he was there mounting a young horse, which evidently had scarcely ever before been saddled, the

creature plunged very violently. Pizarro was evidently
weak from his accident, and, as he fell, the horse kicked
him with both legs on his back.

Still he declared he was not hurt, though he looked
very faint, and could scarcely mount his horse. I galloped
on to the post hut, and waited there more than an hour for
the carriage. At last I saw it coming at a walk, and as soon
as it drove up, Pizarro said he could go no farther. I was
therefore obliged to order another boy as a postilion, and
while they were catching the horses with the lasso, I was
assisting poor Pizarro. I was very sorry to be obliged to
leave him, particularly as he seemed so unwilling to leave
me. I gave him some money, half a bottle of brandy, which
was all I had; and to a woman, who was a few years
younger than Pizarro, and of the same mongrel breed as
himself, I gave two dollars, to rub Pizarro's back three
times a day with the brandy; and I put some salt into it,
that the woman should not drink the brandy, instead of
rubbing Pizarro's back with it. This being all I could do
for him, I mounted my horse, and wishing him good-bye,
to which he replied, "Señor, vaya con Dios," I left him.

I desired the carriage to follow, and I rode from post
to post ordering horses to be ready for the carriage, and
got to San Luis about one o'clock in the morning. I was
completely by myself, without any postilion; but, as it
was a fine moonlight night, and as I had twice before
traveled over the country, I managed to go the right road,
and at five o'clock I again started to ride towards Mendoza.

In the province of Santa Fe, a few of the posts are fortified
to protect the inhabitants against the Indians.

The fort is a very simple one. The huts are surrounded
by a small ditch, which is sometimes fenced on the inside
with a row of prickly pears.

The ditch I have generally been able to jump over on
foot, but no horse of the country would attempt to leap it.

Most of these forts have often been attacked by the

Indians; and one of them I looked at with peculiar interest, as it had very lately been defended for nearly an hour by eight gauchos against about three hundred Indians. The cattle, the women, and six families of little children, were all in the inside, spectators of a contest on which so much depended, and they described their feelings to me with a great deal of nature and expression.

They said that the naked Indians rode up to the ditch with a scream which was quite terrific, and that, finding that they could not cross it, the cacique at last ordered them to get off their horses and pull down the gate. Two had dismounted, when the musket which the gauchos had, and which before had constantly missed fire, went off, and one of the Indians was shot. They then all galloped away; but in a few seconds their cacique led them on again with a terrible cry, and at a pace which was indescribable. They took up their dead comrade and then rode away, leaving two or three of their spears on the ground.

One of these long spears was leaning against the hut, and as the gauchos who had defended the place stood by it, muffled up in their ponchos, with two or three women suckling their infants, several children playing about them, and three or four beautiful girls looking up to them, I thought the spear was one of the proudest military trophies I had ever beheld.

I could never learn that any of these forts had been taken by the Indians, who can do nothing on foot, and whose horses cannot leap; but the ditches are so shallow and so narrow, that by killing a few horses, and tumbling them in, they might in two minutes ride into any part of the place.

I often asked the gauchos why they did not defend themselves in the corral, which at first appeared to me to be a stronger position than the forts; but they said that the Indians often brought lassos of hide, with which they could pull down the stakes of the corral; that sometimes they made a fire against them, and that, besides this, their spears being eighteen feet in length, they were often able to kill every animal in the corral.

The fear which all wild animals in America have of man is very singularly seen in the pampas. I often rode towards the ostriches and gamas, crouching under the opposite side of my horse's neck; but I always found that, although they would allow any loose horse to approach them, they, even when young, ran from me, though little of my figure was visible; and when one saw them all enjoying themselves in such full liberty, it was at first not pleasing to observe that one's appearance was everywhere a signal to them that they should fly from their enemy. Yet it is by this fear that "man hath dominion over the beasts of the field," and there is no animal in South America that does not acknowledge this instinctive feeling.

As a singular proof of the above, and of the difference between the wild beasts of America and of the Old World, I will venture to relate a circumstance which a man sincerely assured me had happened to him in South America.

He was trying to shoot some wild ducks, and, in order to approach them unperceived, he put the corner of his poncho over his head, and crawling along the ground upon his hands and knees, the poncho not only covered his body, but trailed along the ground behind him. As he was thus creeping by a large bush of reeds, he heard a loud sudden noise, between a bark and roar; he felt something heavy strike his feet, and instantly jumping up, he saw, to his astonishment, a large male lion actually standing on his poncho, and perhaps the animal was equally astonished to find himself in the immediate presence of so athletic a man!

The man told me he was unwilling to fire, as his gun was loaded with very small shot, and he therefore stood his ground, and the lion stood on his poncho for many seconds; at last he turned his head, and walking very slowly away about ten yards, he stopped and turned again. The man still stood his ground, upon which the lion tacitly acknowledged his supremacy, and walked off.

After being in the post hut a few minutes, I heard a sigh, and looking into the corner from whence it proceeded, I saw an old sick woman lying on the ground. Her head was resting on a horse's skull, close to a great hole in the wall, and when she earnestly asked me if I had anything "por remedio," I instantly advised her to move herself into a warmer corner. She was feverish and ill, and seemed disappointed at the advice I had given her—she did not understand what the hole in the wall could possibly have to do with her illness, and she again asked me if I had any "remedio."

I had in my waistcoat pocket a little dirty paper parcel of calomel and jalap, which I had promised, much against my will, to carry with me, and which I had already twice carried across the pampas. I did not exactly know how much there was of it, but I had a great mind to shake a little of it into the old woman's mouth, for I thought (as she had certainly never tasted calomel before) it would probably work a miracle within her; however, she was so ill that, upon reflection, I did not feel authorized to give it to her, and besides I thought that if she died I should have to answer for it when I returned, so, partly from conscience and partly from prudence, I left her.

I may observe that this old woman was the only sick person I ever saw in South America. The temperate lives the people lead apparently give them an uninterrupted enjoyment of health, and the list of disorders with which the old world is afflicted is altogether unknown. The beef on which they almost entirely subsist is so lean and tough, that few are tempted to eat more than is necessary, and if a hungry gaucho has swallowed too much of a wild cow, the cure which nature has to perform is very simple. She has only by fever to deprive him of his appetite for a day or two, and he is well again.

I have often remarked that the gaucho has no remedy for any small flesh wound, and does not even keep the dirt from it, for his habit of body is so healthy that the cure is positively going on as he gallops along the plain.

I came to a post, and found horses in the corral, but the men all out. The woman told me they would be in soon, if I would wait. I saw a little child about seven years old, and said I would take him as a postilion. "Bien" (very well), said the woman, upon which the little boy was going to say something, but I took him by the arm, and leading him out to the corral, I caught our horses with a lasso which was lying on the ground.

After we had started, and had ridden about a league, "Oiga, señor," said the little rosy-faced urchin, "yo no soy baquiano" (I do not know the road). I took up my whip and frightened him on before me; but we were shortly overtaken by a man, who had galloped after us from the post as hard as his horse could go. He said he was the boy's father, that there were a number of salteadores in the country—that it was not safe for the child, and that he had therefore come to conduct me. I had ridden more than a hundred miles, was very tired, not at all inclined to talk, and the man steadily galloped on before me. "Vea, señor!" (see!) said the little boy as he frisked by my side, pointing to some wild ducks in a pool, which he wanted me to shoot at with my pistols.

His father was at this moment singing a wild sort of Spanish hymn, and he had just got to the last note, upon which he was to hang for several seconds, when the merry little child, finding that there was no fun in me, loosened his rein, came up with his father, and gave his horse a blow as hard as he was able with the long whip which hung at his bridle, and then laughing, he darted away like a young colt, while his father with the greatest gravity continued the last note of his song.

Arrived at a post hut, and found its owner, Don José, skinning a cow which he had just killed—he was assisted by a black woman of about fifty, who busily continued the operation, while Don José slowly walked towards the corral to catch me a horse.

A pan of muddy water was outside the door, and I tossed a real to the black woman to let me wash my face in it; but when I asked her if there was a piece of looking glass in the hut, she replied with considerable contempt, and without raising her grey woolly head, "Aquí no hay." At this moment a young gaucho, who was playing with some children near the door, recognized me; he had once ridden with me as a postilion, and he now offered to saddle my horse.

I was therefore going to lie down for a few minutes among the long grass to rest myself, when passing the corner of the hut I saw close before me a female figure pounding corn. She was the only daughter and eldest child of Don José (who was a widower), and she was about sixteen years of age. Her whole dress consisted of a coarse woolen petticoat, and over her bare shoulders was loosely thrown (as a shawl) an old scarlet poncho. With a large wooden pestle which she held in both hands, and which she lifted above her head, she was pounding Indian corn in a mortar rudely hewn out of one end of the trunk of a tree, which must have been dragged to the hut, for the purpose, more than a hundred miles. As soon as I appeared before her, with one hand she closed her poncho in front, and continued to pound the corn with the other; however, as soon as I asked her a few questions about the corn, she began earnestly and with great naïveté to explain to me the whole operation, and then working the pestle with both her hands, she illustrated her art both by practice and theory, pounding and expounding at the same time; and although I cared but little how the corn was pounded, yet it was impossible to help admiring the artless simplicity and innocence of the girl's countenance, manners, and appearance. The plain of brown grass extended around us, and the horizon was like the circle which is seen at sea. No cattle were in sight—and in no direction was there anything to arrest the eye, but the hut —the corral—the old blind woman intently skinning the cow—and this girl pounding her corn.

As she was in the middle of her explanation, I interrupted her by observing that "la negra" (the black woman) had told me there was no looking glass in the hut. "No hay, señor," said the girl. What then, said I, have you never seen your own face? "No, señor," she replied, looking down at the corn. I instantly thought whether it would be possible to describe it to her, but "señor! señor! señor!" vociferated the boy as he came from the corral leading my horse.

I therefore at once walked to meet him—but before I mounted my horse, I took a little memorandum book from my pocket, and wrote in it "Black woman skinning a cow," for the rest of the scene I thought I should remember.

I arrived for the night at a hut, where there were fowls, and I begged the woman to cook one of them immediately.

As soon as the water in a large pot had boiled, the woman caught a hen, and killed it by holding its head in her hand; and then, giving the bird two or three turns in the air, to my horror and utter astonishment, she instantly put the fowl into the pot, feathers and all; and although I had resolved to rough it on my journey, yet I positively could not make up my mind to drink such broth or "potage au naturel" as I thought she was preparing for me. I ran to her, and, in very bad Spanish, loudly protested against her cookery; however, she quietly explained to me that she had only put the fowl there to scald it, and as soon as I let go her arm she took it out. The feathers all came off together, but they stuck to her fingers almost as fast as they had before to the fowl. After washing her hands, she took a knife, and very neatly cut off the wings, the two legs, the breast and the back, which she put one after another into a small pot with some beef suet and water, and the rest of the fowl she threw away.

VIII

THE PAMPAS INDIANS

When one compares the relative size of America with the rest of the world, it is singular to reflect on the history of those fellow creatures who are the aborigines of the land; and after viewing the wealth and beauty of so interesting a country, it is painful to consider what the sufferings of the Indians have been, and still may be. Whatever may be their physical or moral character, whether more or less puny in body or in mind than the inhabitants of the old world, still they are the human beings placed there by the Almighty; the country belonged to them, and they are therefore entitled to the regard of every man who has religion enough to believe that God has made nothing in vain, or whose mind is just enough to respect the persons and the rights of his fellow creatures.

A fair description of the Indians I believe does not exist. The Spaniards, on the discovery of the country, exterminated a large proportion of this unfortunate race; the rest they considered as beasts of burden, and during their short intervals of repose, the priests were ordered to explain to them, that their vast country belonged to the Pope at Rome. The Indians, unable to comprehend this claim, and sinking under the burdens which they were doomed to carry, died in great numbers. It was therefore convenient to vote that they were imbecile both in body and in mind; the vote was seconded by the greedy voice of avarice, and carried by the artifices of the designing, and the careless indolence of those who had no interest in the question; it became a statement which historians have now recorded.

But although the inquiry has been thus lulled to rest, and is now the plausible excuse for our total ignorance on the subject, ought not the state of man in America to be infinitely more interesting than descriptions of its mines, its mountains, &c., &c., &c.

During my gallop in America, I had little time or opportunity to see many of the Indians; yet from what I did hear and see of them, I sincerely believe they are as fine a set of men as ever existed under the circumstances in which they are placed. In the mines I have seen them using tools which our miners declared they had not strength to work with, and carrying burdens which no man in England could support; and I appeal to those travelers who have been carried over the snow on their backs, whether they were able to have returned the compliment, and if not, what can be more grotesque than the figure of a civilized man riding upon the shoulders of a fellow creature whose physical strength he has ventured to despise?

The Indians of whom I heard the most were those who inhabit the vast unknown plains of the pampas, and who are all horsemen, or rather pass their lives on horseback. The life they lead is singularly interesting. In spite of the climate, which is burning hot in summer, and freezing in winter, these brave men, who have never yet been subdued, are entirely naked, and have not even a covering for their head.

They live together in tribes, each of which is governed by a cacique, but they have no fixed place of residence. Where the pasture is good, there are they to be found, until it is consumed by their horses, and they then instantly move to a more verdant spot. They have neither bread, fruit, nor vegetables, but they subsist entirely on the flesh of their mares, which they never ride; and the only luxury in which they indulge is that of washing their hair in mare's blood.

The occupation of their lives is war, which they consider is their noble and most natural employment; and they declare that the proudest attitude of the human figure is when, bending over his horse, man is riding at his enemy. The principal weapon which they use is a spear eighteen feet long; they manage it with great dexterity, and are able to give it a tremulous motion which has often shaken the sword from the hand of their European adversaries. From being constantly on horseback, the Indians can scarcely walk. This may seem singular, but from their infancy they are unaccustomed to it. Living in a boundless plain, it may easily be conceived that all their occupations and amusements must necessarily be on horseback, and from riding so many hours the legs become weak, which naturally gives a disinclination to an exertion which every day becomes more fatiguing; besides, the pace at which they can skim over the plains on horseback is so swift, in comparison to the rate they could crawl on foot, that the latter must seem a cheerless exertion.

As a military nation they are much to be admired, and their system of warfare is more noble and perfect in its nature than that of any nation in the world. When they assemble, either to attack their enemies, or to invade the country of the Christians, with whom they are now at war, they collect large troops of horses and mares, and then uttering the wild shriek of war, they start at a gallop. As soon as the horses they ride are tired, they vault upon the bare backs of fresh ones, keeping their best until they positively see their enemies. The whole country affords pasture to their horses, and whenever they choose to stop, they have only to kill some mares. The ground is the bed on which from their infancy they have always slept, and they therefore meet their enemies with light hearts and full stomachs, the only advantages which they think men ought to desire.

How different this style of warfare is to the march of an army of our brave but limping, footsore men, crawling in the rain through muddy lanes, bending under their packs, while in their rear the mules, and forage, and pack-saddles, and baggage, and wagons, and women—bullocks lying on the ground unable to proceed, &c., &c., form a scene of despair and confusion which must always attend the army that walks instead of rides, and that eats cows

instead of horses. How impossible would it be for a
European army to contend with such an aerial force. As
well might it attempt to drive the swallows from the
country, as to harm these naked warriors.

A large body of these Indians twice crossed my path,
as I was riding from Buenos Aires to Mendoza and back
again. They had just had an engagement with the Río
Plata troops, who killed several of them, and these were
lying naked and dead on the plain not far from the road.
Several of the gauchos, who were engaged, told me that
the Indians had fought most gallantly, but that all their
horses were tired, or they could never have been attacked;
the gauchos, who themselves ride so beautifully, all declare that it is impossible to ride with an Indian, for that
the Indians' horses are better than theirs, and also that
they have such a way of urging on their horses by their
cries, and by a peculiar motion of their bodies, that even if
they were to change horses, the Indians would beat them.
The gauchos all seemed to dread very much the Indians'
spears. They said that some of the Indians charged without either bridle or saddle, and that in some instances they
were hanging almost under the bellies of their horses, and
shrieking, so that the horses were afraid to face them. As
the Indians' horses got tired, they were met by fresh troops,
and a great number of them were killed.

To people accustomed to the cold passions of England, it would be impossible to describe the savage, in-
veterate, furious hatred which exists between the gauchos
and the Indians. The latter invade the country for the
ecstatic pleasure of murdering the Christians, and in the
contests which take place between them mercy is unknown. Before I was quite aware of these feelings, I was
galloping with a very fine-looking gaucho, who had been
fighting with the Indians, and after listening to his report
of the killed and wounded, I happened, very simply, to
ask him, how many prisoners they had taken. The man
replied by a look which I shall never forget—he clenched
his teeth, opened his lips, and then sawing his fingers

across his bare throat for a quarter of a minute, bending towards me, with his spurs striking into his horse's side, he said, in a sort of low, choking voice, "Se matan todos" (we kill them all). But this fate is what the Indian firmly expects, and from his earliest youth he is prepared to endure not only death, but tortures, if the fortune of war should throw him alive among his enemies; and yet how many there are who accuse the Indians of that imbecility of mind which in war bears the name of cowardice. The usual cause for this accusation is that the Indians have almost always been known to fly from firearms.

When first America was discovered, the Spaniards were regarded by the Indians as divinities, and perhaps there was nothing which tended to give them this distinction more than their possessing weapons, which, resembling the lightning and the thunder of Heaven, sent death among them in a manner which they could not avoid or comprehend; and although the Christians are no longer considered as divine, yet the Indians are so little accustomed to, or understand the nature of firearms, that it is natural to suppose the danger of these weapons is greater in their minds than the reality.

Accustomed to war among themselves with the lance, it is a danger also that they have not learnt to encounter, and it is well known that men can learn to meet danger, and that they become familiar with its face, when, if the mask be changed, and it appear with unusual features, they again view it with terror. But even supposing that the Indians have no superstitious fear of firearms, but merely consider their positive effects, is it not natural that they should fear them? In Europe, or in England, what will people, with sticks in their hands, do against men who have firearms? Why exactly what the naked Indians have been accused of doing—run away. And who would not run away?

But the life which the Indian leads must satisfy any unprejudiced person that he must necessarily possess high courage. His profession is war, his food is simple, and his body is in that state of health and vigor that he can rise naked from the plain on which he has slept, and proudly look upon his image which the white frost has marked out upon the grass without inconvenience. What can we "men in buckram" say to this?

The life of such a people must certainly be very interesting, and I always regretted very much that I had not time to throw off my clothes and pay a visit to some of the tribes, which I should otherwise certainly have done, as, with proper precautions, there would have been little to fear; for it would have been curious to have seen the young sporting about the plains in such a state of wild nature, and to have listened to the sentiments and opinions of the old; and I would gladly have shivered through the cold nights, and have lived upon mare's flesh in the day, to have been a visitor among them.

From individuals who had lived many years with them, I was informed that the religion of the Pampas Indians is very complicated. They believe in good spirits and bad ones, and they pray to both. If any of their friends die before they have reached the natural term of life (which is very unusual), they consider that some enemy has prevailed upon the evil spirit to kill their friend, and they assemble to determine who this enemy can be. They then denounce vengeance against him. These disputes have very fatal consequences, and have the political effect of alienating the tribes from one another, and of preventing that combination among the Indians which might make them much more dreaded by the Christians.

They believe in a future state, to which they conceive they will be transferred as soon as they die. They expect that they will then be constantly drunk, and that they will always be hunting; and as the Indians gallop over their plains at night, they will point with their spears to constellations in the heavens, which they say are the figures of their ancestors, who, reeling in the firmament, are mounted upon horses swifter than the wind, and are hunting ostriches.

They bury their dead, but at the grave they kill several of their best horses, as they believe that their friend would otherwise have nothing to ride. Their marriages are very simple. The couple to be married, as soon as the sun sets, are made to lie on the ground with their heads towards the west. They are then covered with the skin of a horse, and as soon as the sun rises at their feet, they are pronounced to be married.

The Indians are very fond of any sort of intoxicating liquor, and when they are at peace with Mendoza, and some of the other provinces, they often bring skins of ostriches, hides, &c., to exchange for knives, spurs, and liquor.

The day of their arrival they generally get drunk, but before they indulge in this amusement, they deliberately deliver up to their cacique their knives, and any other weapons they possess, as they are fully aware that they will quarrel as soon as the wine gets into their heads. They then drink till they can hardly see, and fight, and scratch, and bite, for the rest of the evening. The following day they devote to selling their goods, for they never will part with them on the day on which they resolve to be tipsy, as they say that in that state they would be unable to dispose of them to advantage.

They will not sell their skins for money, which they declare is of no use, but exchange them for knives, spurs, maté, sugar, &c. They refuse to buy by weight, which they do not understand; so they mark out upon a skin how much is to be covered with sugar, or anything of the sort which they desire to receive in barter for their property. After their business is concluded, they generally devote another day to Bacchus, and when they have got nearly sober, they mount their horses, and with a loose rein, and with their new spurs, they stagger and gallop away to their wild plains.

Without describing any more of their customs, which I repeat only from hearsay, I must only again lament that the history of these people is not better known; for, from

many facts which I heard concerning them, I really believe that they, as well as the Araucana Indians, possess
many brave and estimable qualities. It is singular, however, to think how mutually they and the inhabitants of
the old world are unacquainted with each other. These
untamed soldiers know nothing of the governments, customs, habits, wants, luxuries, virtues, or follies, of our
civilized world, and what does the civilized world know of
them? It votes them savages *et voilà tout*; but as soon as
firearms shall get into the hands of these brave naked men,
they will tumble into the political scale as suddenly as if
they had fallen from the moon; and while the civilized
world is watching the puny contests of Spaniards who
were born in the old world against their children who
were born in the new one, and is arguing the cause of
dependence versus independence, which in reality is but
a quibble, the men that the ground belongs to will appear,
and we shall then wonder how it is that we never felt for
them, or cared for them, or hardly knew that they existed.

It may to many appear improbable that they should
be ever able to overturn any of the feeble governments
which at present exist; yet these men, without firearms,
and with nothing in their hands but the lance, which is
literally a reed, were twice within fifty leagues of Buenos
Aires while I was in the country, and the montoneros
went among them while I was at San Luis, to offer to arm
them. Besides this, the experience and history of the old
world instruct us that the rise and fall of nations is a subject
far beyond the scrutiny of man, and that, for reasons
which we are unable to comprehend, the wild and de-
spised tribes of our own world have often rushed from the
polar towards the equatorial regions, and like the atmosphere from the north, have chilled and checked the luxury
of the south; and therefore, however ill it may suit our
politics to calculate upon such an event as the union of the
Araucana and Pampas Indians, who can venture to say
that the hour may not be decreed, when these men,
mounted upon the descendants of the very horses which

were brought over the Atlantic to oppress their forefathers, may rush from the cold region to which they have been driven, and with irresistible fury proclaim to the guilty conscience of our civilized world that the hour of retribution has arrived; that the sins of the fathers are visited upon the children; that the descendants of Europeans are in their turn trampled under foot, and, in agony and torture, in vain are asking mercy from the *naked Indians*?

What a lesson this dreadful picture would afford! However, it is neither my profession nor my wish to moralize; but it is impossible for a solitary individual to pass over the magnificent regions of America, without respecting the fellow creatures who were placed there by the Almighty.

IX

ACROSS THE GREAT CORDILLERA

The mules were ordered at twelve o'clock, but did not arrive till four: we had been waiting for them with great impatience; at last we heard the tinkling bell approaching, and they then came into the yard of the fonda, driven by the capataz and one peon. The capataz was a tall stout man, with a bad expression of countenance; we found him cruel, lazy, insolent, cowardly, and careless of everything but eating, and all this easily to be read in his countenance. The peon was a handsome, slight-made, active young fellow.

There were sixteen mules of different sizes and colors; they were all thin, but looked very healthy and hardy. One or two of them had dreadful sore backs, which I pointed out to the capataz, who promised to change them as soon as he got out of Mendoza. As my party consisted of eight people, and as we had baggage sufficient for six mules, we had only two spare ones, and these unable to work; whereas I learned afterwards, that the capataz was bound to provide a much larger proportion of extra mules, but he was as greedy after lucre as he was after food, and to save a few dollars he would have worked his poor mules to death. However, I was then ignorant of the customs of the country, and indeed did not know what was required for the journey I was about to take; and anxious to be off, I ordered the mules to be saddled.

As soon as this was done, the baggage mules were to be got ready. The capataz said he could not load them until every article of baggage was brought into the yard, and accordingly he made a great heap of it. He and the peon then divided it into six parcels, quite different from each other in weight or bulk, but adapted to the strength of the different mules.

74

The operation of loading then began. The peon first caught a great brown mule with his lasso, and he then put a poncho over his eyes, and tied it under his throat, leaving the animal's nose and mouth uncovered. The mule instantly stood still, while the capataz and peon first put on the large straw packsaddle, which they girthed to him in such a manner that nothing could move it. They then placed the articles one by one on each side, and bound them all together, with a force and ingenuity against which it was hopeless for the mule to contend.

One could not help pitying the poor animal, on seeing him thus prepared for carrying a heavy load such a wearisome distance, and over such lofty mountains as the Andes; yet it is truly amusing to watch the nose and mouth of a mule, when his eyes are blinded, and his ears pressed down upon his neck in the poncho. Every movement which is made about him, either to arrange his saddle or his load, is resented by a curl of his nose and upper lip, which in ten thousand wrinkles is expressive, beyond description, of everything that is vicious and spiteful; he appears to be planning all sorts of petty tricks of revenge, and as soon as the poncho is taken off, generally begins to put some of them into execution, either by running with his load against some brother mule, or by kicking him; however, as soon as he finds that his burden is not to be got rid of, he dismisses, or perhaps conceals, his resentment, and instantly assumes a look of patience and resignation, which are really also the characteristics of his race, and which support them under all their sufferings and privations.

As soon as the baggage mules were ready, we took up our pistols and carbines, and after mounting our mules, and shaking hands with the crowd who had assembled in the yard, we bade adieu to the fonda of Mendoza. The last person that I bade farewell to was the old black cook, who was really crying to see us go. She was one of the most warm-hearted and faithful creatures I had ever met with. She came to me just before I started, to beg me to take care of myself, and she was then half-laughing and half-crying. I was at the moment going to throw away a pair of green goggle-spectacles, with shining, lacquered rims, which I had bought to cross the snow of the cordillera, but which I had just condemned as troublesome and useless; however, seeing the old woman's grief, I gave them to her, and put them on the bridge of her short black nose, sticking the ends of them into her woolly hair. She considered it, perhaps, as an act of kindness, and began to cry; and although the group around us were roaring with laughter, the spectacles remained on her nose all the time I was conversing with her. She then took them off, and looking at them with great pride and delight, put them into the bosom of her gown.

The saddling of the mules had taken up so much time that the sun had nearly set. It was still oppressively hot; however, the siesta, which with eating, &c., is in Mendoza an operation of six hours, was over, and the people were standing at their doors to see us pass; but as we went by the alameda road, we soon got out of the town. In the stream which runs along the row of poplars which shade this alameda, or public walk, the people were bathing as usual, without any dresses, and apparently regardless of each other. The young called out to us, and many jokes were taken and given.

After passing the long alameda, the road, for about two leagues, passes through a country artificially irrigated from the Rió Mendoza, and its luxuriance and fertility are quite extraordinary. The brown mud walls which bound the road were covered with grapes, which hung down in beautiful clusters; and the number of peach trees, loaded with fruit, and scattered among rich crops of corn and other agricultural produce, gave the scene an appearance of great luxury and abundance; while the mountains of the cordillera formed a magnificent boundary to a picture which, to one about to cross the Andes, is peculiarly interesting. As soon as the boundary of irrigation is passed, the country ceases to be productive. The soil, light and sandy, produces no sort of herbage, and for more than thirty miles, the road, as it approaches the mountains, passes through a plain, which bears nothing but low stunted shrubs; and when one considers that such has probably been its produce since the creation of the world, it is surprising to see that vegetation, so nearly extinct, should have lingered so long without expiring. However, its existence in these plains proves that they are capable of producing crops for man, whenever his industry will seek for the treasure.

The road across this flat country is always tedious; for the mountains, on leaving Mendoza, appear within three or four miles of the town, and the path seems literally to lengthen as one goes. We found it particularly so, as we had to travel in a night which was unusually dark. The plain before us was not visible, while the black outline of the mountains against the sky appeared close to us, or rather immediately above us. However, we at last got to the first ravine of the cordillera; and then, with the noble mountains towering over our heads, sometimes lost in darkness, and sometimes marked out by the few stars which were visible, we followed the sound of the water, until the distant light at the post hut, and the barking of the dogs as they came rushing towards us, told us that we should now cross the stream, which we did, and then rode up to the post. The dogs continued barking, and occasionally biting at our mules' tails, until the postmaster and another man came to us. They were sleeping by the embers of a fire, in the kitchen or shed which was before us. One side was completely open, the other three were of boughs wattled, but so open that the smoke easily escaped.

The post of Villavicencio, which in all the maps of South America looks so respectable, now consists of a solitary hut without a window, with a bullock's hide for a door, and with very little roof. As the night was cold, I preferred sleeping in the kitchen by the fire, leaving the mules to do as they chose, and to go wherever their fancies might incline them. I took for my pillow one of the horses' skulls, which in South America are used as chairs, and wrapping myself up in my poncho, I dropped off to sleep. When I awoke, which was before daybreak, I found two peons and one of my party asleep round the fire, and a great dog snoring at my back.

I called out for the capataz, who came to me rubbing his eyes, and looking dirty and sleepy, and I told him to go after his mules; but one of the men said that the peon was already gone. Our men were also up, preparing some soup, and as the day began to dawn, and as the mules did not appear, I resolved to find out the baths, which are about a mile off. I followed a path until I came to a spot where I was surrounded by hills, which it seemed quite impossible to climb even on hands and knees; however, on proceeding, I found a singular passage cut in the rock, and climbing up to it, came suddenly to a little spot, in which were the ruins of two or three huts, and three or four tents.

The huts and the tents were swarming with people, and the discovery of twenty or thirty fellow creatures in such a sequestered spot was altogether unexpected. They had come there from great distances for the purpose of bathing, and many of them I afterwards learned were very respectable people. As I had no time to lose, and wanted to bathe, I asked a man who was looking out of a tent, where the baths were. With the indifference and in-dolence usual in the country, he made no reply, but he pointed with his chin to some little walls close before him, two- or three-feet high, built with loose stones and in ruins. I was also close to them, so I took off my jacket and my belt of pistols, and walked towards them; but not believing they could be baths, I looked towards the man, and asked him if they were there. He made with his head the usual sign of "sí"; so I walked towards the walls, and to my astonishment I found a hole a little bigger than a coffin, with a woman lying in it! Seeing that there was no room for me there, I reconnoitered the spot, and found another hole about ten yards above the lady, and another about the same distance below her. As the water ran from the one to the other, I thought I might as well act the part of the wolf as be the lamb, and I therefore went up the stream, and got into the upper bath. I found the water very hot and agreeable; and without troubling myself about its analysis, drank some from the spot where it issued from the ground, and feeling that I had then given it a fair trial, I set off to return. In passing the huts and the tents I looked into them; they were crowded with men, women, and children, of all ages, and mingled together in a way which would not altogether be admitted at our English bathing places; but among the Andes customs and ideas are different, and if a lady has there the rheumatism, she sees no harm in trying to wash it away by the waters of Villavicencio.

As soon as I got back to the post hut I found the mules all saddled; so, after drinking some soup and eating a piece of the hind leg of a guanaco, I set off for Uspallata, where it was proposed we should sleep.

The road, on leaving Villavicencio, instantly turns up a ravine, which is one of the finest passes in the cordillera. The mountains are extremely steep on both sides, and, as the ravine winds in many directions, one often comes to a spot which has the appearance of a cul-de-sac, from which there is no exit to be seen. In some places the rock hangs perpendicularly overhead, and the enormous fragments which nearly block up the road, contrasted with those which appear to be on the point of falling, add to the danger and to the grandeur of the scene. As we were passing, we saw a guanaco on the very highest summit of one of the mountains. He was there evidently for safety; and as he stood against the blue sky, his attitude, as he earnestly watched us, was very expressive of his wild free life; and his small head and thin neck denoted the speed with which he was about to save himself.

I had ridden on by myself about fifteen miles, and had gained, by a constant ascent, the summit of the Paramillo, the high range of mountains which overhang Villavicencio. The view from this point is very interesting. The ground continues level for a short distance, and then rapidly descends towards the valley of Uspallata, which is about thirty miles off.

This valley is the upper base of the great range of the cordilleras; and it is, at first, surprising to see that the hills of the Paramillo, which had appeared so lofty, are very humble features compared with the stupendous barrier which, in spite of its distance, appears to be on the point of obstructing the passage.

This enormous mass of stone, for it appears to be perfectly barren, is so wild and rude in its features and construction that no one would judge that any animal could force its way across the summit, which, covered with snow, in some places eternal, seems to be a region between the heavens and the practicable habitation of man; and indeed to attempt to pass it, except by following up in a ravine the course of a torrent, would be altogether impossible.

From the Paramillo, the view on the east, or contrary direction, is also very interesting. It is pleasing to look down on the difficulties which have been surmounted even to gain this point; and beyond is a vast expanse of what, at first, very much resembles the ocean, but which one soon recognizes as the vast plains of Mendoza and the pampas.

The natural exhalation from the earth covers them with a cloud of uncertainty; places which one has heard talked of as points of importance are lost in space, and the hopes and passions and existence of mankind are buried in the atmosphere which supports them. But one has not much time for moralizing on the summit of the Paramillo, for it is such a windy spot that a man's most rational exertion there is to hold on his hat; and as the large broad-brimmed one which I had purchased at Mendoza made several attempts to return there, I and my mule proceeded towards the valley of Uspallata. After going a league or two, I observed on both sides of me large tawny-colored fungus-looking substances, which in size, shape, and color so resembled lions lying on the ground that sometimes I really could not distinguish whether they were or not.

In the pampas I had always observed the singular manner in which all animals, particularly birds, are there protected from their enemies by plants or foliage which resemble them; and as I knew there were a great number of lions about Villavicencio, and could see the track of their large feet in my path, I began to think that some of them were really lying before me. However, it seemed foolish to stop, and therefore I continued for some time; at last, coming to a small coppery vein in the rock, I thought it would be a good excuse to inspect it, so I remained there cracking the stones till two of my party came up, and their first observation to me was, how very like the substances around us were to lions.

One of the party had a horse's leg in his hand. He told me that he had never been so tired in his life; that his mule, in mounting the hill, had become quite exhausted; and that, when he got off to lead her, she would not follow him: that, in despair, he made her drink up his flask of brandy, and that then, taking as a whip a dried-up horse's leg that was lying on the ground, he remounted the mule, which had gone very well ever since. "But, sir," said my honest companion, "whether it be the brandy that has got into her head, or the notion of being beaten with a horse's leg that has urged her on, I cannot tell you."

We continued our course together, and descending the hill, came to the district in which the Uspallata mines are situated. The climate of the country in which those mines are situated is what would naturally be expected from its latitude and elevation. The former places it under a hot sun, the latter imparts to it a considerable degree of cold; and as the air is both dry and rarefied, there is little refraction, and consequently the heat and light of day vanish almost as soon as the sun is below the horizon. In visiting these mines in winter we found the days hotter than the summer in England, when at night the water constantly froze hard by our sides as we slept crowded together in the small hut. The whole of the country is the most barren I ever witnessed, and from this singular cause, that it never rains there. Without attempting to explain the cause of this phenomenon, the following are some of the facts on which the statement is founded:

1. The huts at several of the mines are built exactly across the ravine, in such a manner that if water was ever to come down the ravine, it must necessarily pass though the huts, or over them.

2. One of the lodes runs up the bottom of a ravine, and the old shafts which are formed in it are in the natural drain of the ravine. These shafts at bottom are dry, and have no appearance of having contained water.

3. The miner, who, to keep possession of the mines, had lived there alone for two years, told us, that during that time it had not rained once.

The soil consists of the decomposed rock, which remains on the steep surface of the mountain, and rolls from under the foot like the loose cinders of Etna and Vesuvius; there is no herbage of any sort or kind upon it. A few low, resinous shrubs are scattered about; but, from the severity of the climate, in most places they grow along the ground. The dead animals which are lying about are all dried-up in their skins, and have a most singular appearance; indeed the whole scene is a very striking example of what a desert the earth would be without water. One of the Cornish miners, after gazing about him with astonishment, took up a handful of the green barren soil, and looking into it with great attention, he said, "Why, surely there must be poison in this ground!"

We had scarcely passed the mines when the sun set, and although we saw the post hut of Uspallata, yet we had great difficulty in reaching it. The rest of the party were lost, and did not arrive till midnight. My first object was to get something for our poor mules; there was very little in the plain except hot stones and resinous shrubs, but I learnt from the man that he had a potrero (or enclosed field) full of grass; he began a long story about how much I was to pay—however, I cut him very short, and sent him off with the mules, who, poor things, were no doubt delighted with their unexpected supper.

We then earnestly inquired of the man what he had for us to eat. And as we all three stood round him, our earnest and greedy looks were an amusing contrast to the calm tranquillity with which he replied "No hay," to everything we asked for; at last we found out that he had dry peaches and live goats. We put some of the former into a pot to boil, and in process of time the boy, who was sent out on horseback with a lasso to catch a goat, arrived. The little fellow could not kill it, and the man was gone for wood; so partly to put an end to the animal's fears, and partly because I was very hungry, I put a pistol to his ear, and in a short time he was roasting on the burning embers.

At this moment an English lady, a child about seven years old, two or three younger ones, and a party of peons arrived. They had, with no other protection, passed the cordillera, and had ridden for twelve or fourteen hours that day in order to get to Uspallata.

The situation of a countrywoman with a family of little children interested us very much, and it was pleasing to hear that they had crossed the cordillera without any accident. The eldest child, who was a very fine boy, had ridden the whole way, but the other little chubby-faced creatures had each been carried upon a pillow in front of the peons' saddles.

In the history of the hut of Villavicencio I had often heard that, in spite of its desert situation and want of comfort, an English lady, who was passing with her husband to Chile about seven or eight years ago, had been confined there, and had remained there until she and her little infant were capable of prosecuting their perilous journey; and when I saw the wretched abode, I had often felt how cheerless it must have been for her to have remained there so long.

The lady who now came to Uspallata was the very

person whose singular sufferings I have described, and the fine little boy was the child that was born at Villavicencio. He had been in Chile ever since, and now the little manly fellow had ridden across the cordillera, and was about to introduce his brothers and sisters to the wild hovel in which it had been decreed that he should be born.

In the morning, before daybreak, we made preparations for starting. Some part of the goat was to form our breakfast; we had some tea with us, and I was very anxious to get some milk, but when I asked the man, he replied, "Leche no hay," with a look that seemed to doubt there being any in the universe. The cows, he said, were four leagues off, and that they would not come for a couple of hours. "Have the goats no milk?" asked I; the fellow laughed at the idea; however, I found out that they had kids, and I therefore insisted on his sending the boy for a she-goat. This order was complied with, and in a short time the boy came, dragging a poor creature with his lasso. She was altogether scared, and was leaping and jumping to get away; however, our peons helped, and she was thrown down upon her side. One peon knelt upon her head, and one of our men held her hind legs, while the boy milked her on one side, and then turning her round, in spite of her struggles, she was milked on the other side. They then let her go, and happy was she at regaining her liberty, after being scared at the uncouth operation she had just undergone.

The mules were now nearly laden, when one of the Cornish miners told me that the capataz wanted to put baggage upon the mule which had got a sore back, and which, according to his agreement, he ought to have changed at Mendoza. I instantly went to the capataz, and found him with his long knife in his hand, actually cutting the poor creature's back, preparatory to putting on the packsaddle. I told him to desist, but he was explaining to me how he was going to place the saddle, so that it should not hurt the mule, and he was just going to put on a small straw pad, when I at once put an end to the argument. As soon as the baggage was ready, we threw upon it two or three dead sheep, and, in quitting Uspallata, took leave of the last inhabited hut on the east side of the cordillera.

I was steadily riding my mule at the rate of five miles an hour, in order to measure by my watch the breadth of the plains of Uspallata, when we met an old gaucho huntsman, with two lads, and a number of dogs, which at once put a stop to my calculation. He had several loose horses, over one of which was hanging the carcass of a guanaco.

He had been hunting for lions, and had been among the mountains for two days, but had had little sport. The gaucho was a fine picture of an old sportsman. Round his body were the boleadoras (balls), which were covered with clotted blood. His knees were admirably protected from the bushes by a hide which was under his saddle, and which in front had the appearance of gambadoes.

He was mounted on a good horse, his lasso in coils hung at his saddle. As soon as we stopped, he was surrounded by his dogs, which were a very odd pack. Some of them were very large, and some quite small, and they seemed to be all of different breeds; many had been lamed by the lions and tigers, and several bore honorable scars. I regretted very much indeed that I had not time to follow the sport, which must have been highly interesting.

As soon as the dogs unkennel a lion or a tiger, they pursue him until he stops to defend himself. If the dogs fly upon him, the gaucho jumps off his horse, and while the animal is contending with his enemies, he strikes him on the head with the balls, to which an extraordinary momentum can be given. If the dogs are at bay, and afraid to attack their foe, the gaucho then hurls the lasso over him, and galloping away, he drags him along the ground, while the hounds rush upon him and tear him.

The mountains now seemed to be really over our heads, and we expected that we should have immediately to climb them, but for many hours we went over a plain as dry and barren as the country already described on the other side of Uspallata, and which wound its course among the mountains. At last we crossed a rapid torrent of water, and then immediately afterwards came to another, which takes its rise at the summit of the Andes, and whose course and comparatively gradual descent directs the passage; and it is on this spot that the traveler may proudly feel that he is at last buried among the mountains of the Andes. The surface of the rocks which surrounded us afforded no pasture, and the gnarled wood and the stunted growth of the trees announced the severity of the climate in winter; yet the forms of the mountains, and the wild groups in which they stood towering one above another can only be viewed with astonishment and admiration.

Although the sun was retiring, and the mules very tired, we wished to have gone on half an hour longer, but the peon assured us we should not find so good a place, and pointing to some withered herbage, and some large loose stones, he earnestly advised me to stop, saying, "Hay aquí pasto bueno para las mulas, y para su merced buen aloja-miento, hay agua, aquí hay todo" (here is pasture for the mules, and for your excellency good lodging, water, and everything). We therefore dismounted near a spring, and having collected wood, and the miners having cooked our supper, we lay down on the ground to sleep. The air was cool and refreshing, and the scene really magnificent.

As I lay on the ground upon my back, the objects around me gradually became obscure, while the sun, which had long ago set to us, still gilded the summits of the highest mountains, and gave a sparkling brightness to the snow which faded with the light of day. The scene underwent a thousand beautiful changes; but when it was all lost in utter darkness, save the bold outline which rested against the sky, it appeared more beautiful than ever.

The peon, who was always very active, was up long before daybreak, and we were awakened by the bell mule and the others which were now collected. We got up in the dark, and as our party were preparing to start, the group, though indistinctly seen by the blaze of the fire, was a very odd one. The three miners were eating their breakfasts seated on loose stones round a large fragment of rock, which served as a table. Their elbows were squared, and they were eagerly bending over the food before them. The peons, with their dark brown faces, and different colored caps, handkerchiefs, and ponchos, were loading the carga mules. Some of the party were putting on their spurs; others were arranging their toilette. The light was now faintly dawning on the tops of the highest mountains, and the snow was just discovered lying in large patches and ridges. The bottoms of the ravines were in dark shade, and white windy clouds were flying across the deep blue sky—for some moments all was silent; however, as soon as the mules were ready we mounted, and we were off before we could distinctly see; but the mules picked their way, and continually ascending by a path covered with great stones, and impracticable to any animal except a mule, we continued to follow the course of the great stream, which was a torrent, roaring and raging, and altogether impassable.

The sufferings of the poor mules now attracted our attention; they had traveled from Mendoza with but little rest, and little food; still they required no driving, but were evidently making every possible exertion to keep up with the mule which carried the bell. Occasionally the carga would require adjusting, and the peon, throwing his poncho over the creature's eyes, would alter it, while the rest continued their course, but the poncho was no sooner removed than the mule, trotting and braying, joined the troop, never stopping till he came to the bell.

On the road, the number of dead mules, which indeed strew the path from Mendoza to Santiago, seemed to increase, and it was painful to see the living ones winding their path among the bones and carcasses of those who had died of fatigue. By the peculiar effect of the climate, most of these poor creatures were completely dry, and as they lay on the road with their hind legs extended, and their heads stretched towards their goal, it was evident from

their attitudes that they had all died of the same complaint
—the hill had killed them all.

After passing one or two very rapid torrents, we came
to a mountain which was one precipitous slope from the
top to the torrent beneath. About half way up, we saw a
troop of forty guanacos, who were all gazing at us with
great attention. They were on a path, or track, parallel to
the water, and as the side of the mountain was covered
with loose stones, we were afraid they would roll some of
them down upon us.

On the opposite side of the water, was one of the most
singular geological formations which we had witnessed. At
the head of a ravine was an enormous perpendicular
mountain of porphyry, broken into battlements and tur-
rets, which gave it exactly the appearance of an old castle,
on a scale, however, altogether, the subject of a romance.
The broken front represented, in a most curious manner,
old-fashioned windows and gates, and one of the Cornish
miners declared "he could see an old woman coming
across a drawbridge."

As I was looking up at the region of snow, and as my
mule was scrambling along the steep side of the rock, the
capataz overtook me, and asked me if I chose to come on,
as he was going to look at the "ladera de las vacas," to see
if it was passable, before the mules came to it. (When
first, from the melting of the snow, the cordillera is "open,"
this passage is always impassable; but it becomes broader
towards the end of summer.) He accordingly trotted on,
and in half an hour arrived at the spot. It is the worst pass
in the cordillera. The mountain above appears almost
perpendicular, and in one continued slope down to the
rapid torrent which is raging underneath. The surface is
covered with loose earth and stones which have been
brought down by the water. The path goes across this
slope, and is very bad for about seventy yards, being only
a few inches broad; but the point of danger is a spot where
the water which comes down from the top of the mountain
either washes the path away, or covers it over with loose

stones. We rode over it, and it certainly was very narrow and bad. In some places the rock almost touches one's shoulder, while the precipice is immediately under the opposite foot, and high above the head are a number of large loose stones, which appear as if the slightest touch would send them rolling into the torrent beneath, which is foaming and rushing with great violence. However, the danger to the rider is only imaginary, for the mules are so careful, and seem so well aware of their situation, that there is no chance of their making a false step. As soon as we had crossed the pass, which is only seventy yards long, the capataz told me that it was a very bad place for baggage mules, that four hundred had been lost there, and that we should also very probably lose one; he said, that he would get down to the water at a place about a hundred yards off, and wait there with his lasso to catch any mule that might fall into the torrent, and he requested me to lead on his mule. However, I was resolved to see the tumble, if there was to be one, so the capataz took away my mule and his own, and while I stood on a projecting rock at the end of the pass, he scrambled down on foot, till he at last got to the level of the water.

The drove of mules now came in sight, one following another; a few were carrying no burdens, but the rest were either mounted or heavily laden, and as they wound along the crooked path, the difference of color in the animals, the different colors and shapes of the baggage they were carrying, with the picturesque dress of the peons, who were vociferating the wild song by which they drive on the mules, and the sight of the dangerous path they had to cross formed altogether a very interesting scene.

As soon as the leading mule came to the commencement of the pass, he stopped, evidently unwilling to proceed, and of course all the rest stopped also.

He was the finest mule we had, and on that account had twice as much to carry as any of the others; his load had never been relieved, and it consisted of four portmanteaus, two of which belonged to me, and which contained not only a very heavy bag of dollars, but also papers which were of such consequence that I could hardly have continued my journey without them. The peons now redoubled their cries, and leaning over the sides of their mules, and picking up stones, they threw them at the leading mule, who now commenced his journey over the path. With his nose to the ground, literally smelling his way, he walked gently on, often changing the position of his feet, if he found the ground would not bear, until he came to the bad part of the pass, where he again stopped, and I then certainly began to look with great anxiety at my portmanteaus; but the peons again threw stones at him, and he continued his path, and reached me in safety; several others followed. At last a young mule, carrying a portmanteau, with two large sacks of provisions, and many other things, in passing the bad point, struck his load against the rock, which knocked his two hind legs over the precipice, and the loose stones immediately began to roll away from under them; however his forelegs were still upon the narrow path. He had no room to put his head there, but he placed his nose on the path on his left, and appeared to hold on by his mouth. His perilous fate was soon decided by a loose mule who came, and in walking along after him, knocked his comrade's nose off the path, destroyed his balance, and head over heels the poor creature instantly commenced a fall which was really quite terrific. With all his baggage firmly lashed to him, he rolled down the steep slope, until he came to the part which was perpendicular, and then he seemed to bound off, and turning round in the air, fell into the deep torrent on his back, and upon his baggage, and instantly disappeared. I thought, of course, that he was killed; but up he rose, looking wild and scared, and immediately endeavored to stem the torrent which was foaming about him. It was a noble effort; and for a moment he seemed to succeed, but the eddy suddenly caught the great load which was upon his back, and turned him completely over; down went his head with all the baggage, and as he was carried down the stream, all I saw were his hind-quarters, and his long, thin, wet tail, lashing the water. As suddenly, however, up his head came again; but he was now weak, and went down the stream, turned round and round by the eddy, until, passing the corner of the rock, I lost sight of him. I saw, however, the peons, with their lassos in their hands, run down the side of the torrent for some little distance; but they soon stopped, and after look-ing towards the poor mule for some seconds, their earnest attitude gradually relaxed, and when they walked to-wards me, I concluded that all was over. I walked up to the peons, and was just going to speak to them, when I saw at a distance a solitary mule walking towards us!

We instantly perceived that he was the Phaeton whose fall we had just witnessed, and in a few moments he came up to us to join his comrades. He was of course dripping wet; his eye looked dull, and his whole counte-nance was dejected; however, none of his bones were bro-ken, he was very little cut, and the bulletin of his health was altogether incredible.

With that surprising anxiety which the mules all have to join the troop, or rather the leading mule which carries the bell, he continued his course, and actually walked over the pass without compulsion, although certainly with great caution.

We then continued our course for two hours, until we came to the Río de las Vacas, which is the most dan-gerous torrent of any of those which are to be crossed. We got through it with safety, but it was very deep, and so excessively rapid that large stones were rolled down it with the force of the water. The mules are accustomed to these torrents, but they are, notwithstanding, much fright-ened at them, and it is only long spurs that can force them into them.

While we were crossing, the peons stood down the stream, with their lassos hurling round their heads, in order to catch anything which might have been carried away; but as the boxes which I had seen washed from the mules were dashed to pieces before they had got twenty yards, the peon's lasso came a little too late; and besides this, as the mule is their own property, I used sometimes to think that, in the hurry and indecision of the moment, they would probably catch him instead of the rider.

When a large party cross this river, and when it is deep, it is really amusing, after one has got across it, to observe the sudden change of countenance of one's friends as *they* ride through it; sometimes perched up on the top of a fragment of rock barely covered, and expecting the next step to be their last; and sometimes scrambling out of a hole, with uplifted eyebrows, open mouth, and an earnest expression of uneasiness and apprehension—and these are really situations into which the traveler in the Andes is often thrown, though they disconcert the gravity and solemnity of his "Personal Narrative."

After passing the Río de las Vacas, the ravines appear to grow narrower and steeper, and the tops of the mountains, which are those of the highest range, are rugged, with sharp edges and pinnacles.

We here came to a quantity of snow and rubbish, which had been washed down, and which we had great difficulty to pass, for it occasionally broke under the weight of the mules, who recovered themselves in a surprising manner, and as if accustomed to it.

We now passed one of the brick huts, which, at every two or three leagues, have been built to protect the traveler from the dreadful storms which here assail him, and after continuing our course till the sun was low, we stopped at the second of these huts.

We saw a party of loose mules at some distance, standing among the stones; and leaving my mule at the hut, I walked to them, and found two or three arrieros on the ground asleep.

I leaned over one fat fellow, and asked him to give me something to eat, for we had lost all our provisions at the ladera de las vacas. As he awoke, he seemed at first alarmed at seeing a stranger well armed so near him; however, we soon came to an understanding, and in a few seconds he was putting some money into a long purse, while I was walking towards the hut, with my arms filled with hard sea biscuits, some dried beef (charqui) with one hand full of salt, and in the other red chili pepper.

With this our men prepared a good dinner, while I reconnoitered our situation. It was barren and desolate beyond description; and the mules, now unsaddled, were standing in the attitudes in which they had been unladen —their heads were nodding, or drooping, and they were putting up their backs and going to sleep, which was the only comfort they could enjoy, for there was literally nothing for them to eat.

The snow was all around us, and the features of the scene so large that one could not but reflect on the situation of the many travelers, who, in these parts of the Andes, have been overtaken by the storm, and have perished.

The capataz told me that these temporales are so violent that no animal can live in them; that there is no warning, but that all of a sudden the snow is seen coming over the tops of the mountains in a hurricane of wind; that hundreds of people have been lost in these storms; that several had been starved in the house before us; and that only two years ago, the winter, by suddenly setting in, as it generally does, had shut up the cordillera, and had driven ten poor travelers to this hut. When the violence of the first storms had subsided, the courier came to the spot, and found six of the ten lying dead in the hut, and by their sides the other four almost dead with hunger and cold. They had eaten their mules and their dog, and the bones of these animals were now before us.

These houses are all erected upon one plan, and are extremely well adapted to their purpose. They are of brick and mortar, and are built solid, ten or twelve feet high, with a brick staircase outside. The room which is on the top of this foundation, in order to raise it above the snow, is about twelve feet square; the walls are extremely thick, with two or three small loop-holes about six inches square; the roof is arched, and the floor is of brick.

A place so small, of so massive a construction, necessarily possesses the character of a dungeon; and, as one stands at the door, the scene around adds a melancholy gloom to its appearance, and one cannot help thinking how sad it must have been, to have seen the snow, day after day, getting deeper and deeper, and the hope of escaping hourly diminishing, until it was evident that the path was impracticable and that the passage was closed! But without these reflections, the interior is melancholy enough.

The table, which had been fixed into the mortar, was torn away; and to obtain a momentary warmth, the wretched people who had been confined here had, in despair, burned the very door which was to protect them from the elements. They had then, at the risk of their lives, taken out the great wooden lintel, which was over the door, and had left the wall above it hanging merely from the adhesion of the mortar. This operation had evidently been done with no instrument but their knives, and it must have been a work of many days.

The state of the walls was also a melancholy testimony of the despair and horror they had witnessed. In all the places which I have ever seen, which have been visited by travelers, I have always been able to read the names and histories of some of those who have gone before me; for when a man has nothing to lament, but that his horses have not arrived, or in fact that he has nothing to do, the wall appears to be a friend to whom many intrust their names, their birthplaces, the place they propose to visit, and sometimes even the fond secrets of their hearts; but I particularly observed that, in these huts on the Andes, not a name was to be seen, or a word upon the walls. Those who had died in them were too intent upon their own sufferings; the horror of their situation was unspeakable, and thus these walls remain the silent monuments of past misery.

As the air was very cold, and the wind very high, we slept in this hut, and before daybreak we were once again upon our poor jaded mules, in order to cross the cumbre, while the surface of the snow was hard from the night's frost. After climbing a little but very steep hill, we came upon a small flat landing place, which was the most dreary looking spot I think I ever saw. I asked the peon what the wooden cross before us meant. After looking over each of his shoulders, he told me that the spot for many years was haunted by the ghost of a mulish-looking sort of man who used to terrify all the arrieros and peons who passed, and that they, therefore, had been absolutely obliged to get a priest to put up the cross before us. "And has that driven the ghost away?" said I, laughing. "Sí," said the peon, with a look of confidence and courage which had rather deserted his face while he was describing the shape of the specter; and he then assured me with great earnestness, "that now he was never seen, and that I need not be afraid."

The torrent which we had so long followed, now turned up the ravine to the right. We had pursued it from the east towards the west, but our path was now obstructed by the cumbre, or upper ridge of the cordillera, which no artifice can avoid, and which is a mountain covered with loose, decomposed rock, at an angle of very nearly forty-five degrees. At the foot is another of the huts, without door, table, or lintel, and in which many people have died.

After resting my mule for a short time, and then girthing my saddle as tight as possible, during which operation he was always trying to bite me, I whispered a little comfort into his long ear; I mounted, and then squaring my shoulders and giving a kick or two with my spurs, I commenced the climb, followed by the party of riders and carga mules.

The path ascended in zigzags from the bottom to the top, and the whole time I was obliged to hold on by the thin mane of the mule. The turnings were so short that the animal was almost falling backwards; however, on he went, with a determination and patience that was quite astonishing. At times he stopped, but the path was so steep, and the decomposed rock so loose, that of his own accord in a few seconds he continued. It was very picturesque and interesting to see the whole party beneath, threading their way in different paths above each other; some going towards the north, and others towards the south—to see the riders leaning forwards, every animal straining to his utmost, and to hear the peons cheering on their mules by a song which was both wild and melodious.

After climbing in this singular manner for about an hour, I reached the summit, and it was really a moment of great triumph and satisfaction. Hitherto I had always been looking upwards, but now the difficulties were all overcome, and I was able to look down upon the mountains. Their tops were covered with snow; and as the eye wandered over the different pinnacles, and up the white trackless ravines, one could not but confess that the scene, cheerless and inhospitable as it was, was nevertheless a picture both magnificent and sublime.

Proceeding among some broken ground along the summit, I saw a very large wooden cross, which I rode up to. It was supported by a heap of stones piled round the bottom of it, but it did not stand perpendicular. It was roughly hewn, mortised together, and fixed by a large spike nail, which had rusted the wood, and being loosely clinched, the cross creaked with the wind. There was a rough inscription, cut out with a knife, along the bar of the cross; but it was so much above my head, and so bleached by the weather, that I could not read it. In the wild desolate situation in which it stood, it certainly looked very appropriate and interesting, and I stood at the foot of it leaning over my mule until the party came up; and then the peon told me that it was placed there by two arrieros to commemorate the murder of their friend. Thus reminded that we had not yet risen above the bad passions of man, it was painful to see the emblem of his hopes standing as the monument of his guilt!

We now found it extremely cold; the snow was very deep, and the mules' path a most extraordinary one. A deep narrow passage had been cut by the constant traveling of these animals, but the wall of snow on each side obliged the rider to put his feet on the mule's ears; besides this, as they always tread on the same spot, every step was into a hole which was often above their knees. On the snow there was a great deal of blood from mules which had gone before, and it was only astonishing that they could proceed at all.

"What a magnificent view!" said I to one of my companions, whose honest heart and thoughts were always faithful to old England. "What thing can be more beautiful?" I added. After smiling for some seconds, he replied, "Them things, sir, that do wear caps and aprons."

After descending about a mile with great trouble and difficulty, we came to another of the huts, which was in the same state as all the rest, but surrounded by about twelve feet of snow; for on the Chile side of the Andes there is always much more snow than on the other. After passing this house we resolved to quit the path, which was getting more bloody and more difficult, and we attempted to take a nearer cut by riding over the snow, which was everywhere very deep. It bore us very well for some time; but as we got lower down, and as the heat of the day increased, our mules began to sink into it; however, they managed to regain the path, except the poor brown mule who was carrying the four heavy portmanteaus. He had hitherto surmounted every difficulty, and with a healthy eye and a patient countenance had always led the way; but now his treacherous path was breaking under him, and after floundering on in a most extraordinary manner, literally raising himself by his nose, he could proceed no farther, and the portmanteaus at his side all rested on the snow. Before this the capataz and peon had only cheered him by their voices, but they now went to his assistance. They lifted up his two forelegs out of the holes which they had made, and they put them on the surface of the snow. They then went on each side, and with one hand on his tail, and the other under his belly, the poor creature rose. The two men then instantly jumped behind the mule, and with their hands over their heads they both held the mule's tail, pushing it upwards with all their force. The weight of the baggage being thus partly supported, the mule was able to proceed, and it was really curious to see the gravity and caution with which the party regained the road.

During this singular operation, one of the party was for a long time endeavoring to catch his mule, who had escaped, and who managed just to keep out of his reach. When his master ran he ran; he followed his example when he walked, and at last, when my companion threw himself down on the snow quite exhausted, the cunning creature stood still and looked at him.

As I found that my mule still went very well, I cut across the snow, and saved more than a mile, though I had some places to descend which no animal but a mule could have accomplished. The melting of the snow had in some places undermined it, and as I traveled over the surface I could hear a torrent rushing under the feet of the mule. Several times I got off to walk, but was obliged to re-mount, as these animals will not be led by the bridle. My mule was getting tired, his back was rather sore, and so were his feet, when I came to a stream of water about a foot broad, but deep, and which was running under the snow we were crossing. The snow had fallen into this stream in two or three places, both above and below me, and I was quite sure it would not bear; so, in order that the mule should tumble by himself, I rode to the very edge and then, dismounting, put the bridle over his neck, and crossing the little stream, I endeavored to persuade him to follow me, but he would not think of it; it was but one step, yet he would not make it.

I then resolved to back him over it, and accordingly taking hold of the mameluke bit which was in his mouth, I tried to turn him round. He would open his mouth, and allow his head to come round to his shoulder, but he knew what I wanted, and nothing could persuade him to move his legs.

I could bear it no longer, so without a witness but the wild mountains about me, I beat him on his nose; however, it was no use, he would not move, and he looked so placid that I could not long be angry with him, and therefore I gave the point up and mounted him. The moment I was on his back, he walked on; as I expected, the snow broke in, and down he fell upon his nose; however, he floundered through it, and then continued as patient as if nothing had happened, sometimes pricking up his ears and looking at his path, as if some great curiosity or some great danger, was before him, and then stopping to bray after his companions, during which nothing would induce him to proceed.

In about an hour we got out of the snow, and then continually descending, the country soon began to assume a different appearance; and when we afterwards came to the first trees, we fancied that we were beholding a most beautiful country, and our whole party were making repeated observations on the particular charms of the scenery, and were pointing out spots which they agreed would be the most delightful situations for villages and cottages.

In returning from several expeditions which we had before made to mountains, to inspect mines, I had always observed how very beautiful the plains looked after a short absence from vegetation, and I endeavored to keep the observation in mind in viewing the scenes before me. Yet, upon the most deliberate reflection, I was of opinion that the climate was lovely, and that although the ground was rocky, the trees had a verdure and a luxuriance that I could not sufficiently admire; but when we returned over these same spots, after living in Chile, we all acknowledged the erroneous opinions we had formed, and were surprised to find the climate severe, the country bleak, and vegetation stunted by the continual frosts and violent winds.

I was now joined by two of my party, and we proceeded along a stream whose course guided us as on the other side. The torrent, however, was much more rapid, and it was very pleasing to see it rushing in a contrary direction to that which we had so long followed. We were riding close to a very high perpendicular mountain which was on our right, and were all looking up it, and making remarks upon its singular formation, when we heard a sound like the sudden explosion of a mine, and a large piece of the rock was instantly seen falling. The sound was exactly like that described, but I should think it must have proceeded from the rock having struck against some part of the cliff; however one of the party exclaimed "Oh! it is all coming!" and off he darted.

The other and I stood still, and we were much amused with the appearance of the fugitive, who bending over his mule, as if the mountain had already been on his shoulders, was kicking and spurring and beating his mule, and in this attitude actually rode out of our sight, without once turning to look behind him.

When we came up to him, "What, did you not see," said he "the whole face of the mountain moving, and smoke piping out of all the crevices?" He added he had heard that Chile was full of volcanoes, that he considered the whole mountain was coming upon him, and that therefore he certainly did ride for his very life.

As our mules were very tired with the fatigue they had undergone in climbing the cumbre, we stopped earlier than usual, at an uninhabited house called La Guardia, where there was some food for the mules, but as the house was full of fleas, most of us slept on the ground outside. A little after midnight, as soon as the moon was up, we again mounted our mules, but as the capataz was very slow in loading the cargas, I rode on with one of the party.

We came to several torrents and laderas, and the former in the dark were passed very unwillingly, for, as my companion very justly said, "If one is to be carried away, one would like to see where one is going." As soon as the sun was up, we found it oppressively hot; and as our mules were getting lame, we could only trot very gently. The country down which we descended was similar to that which has already been described, and we continued our course till we came in sight of the town of Villa Nueva de los Andes, whose name explains that it is a new town built in the Andes.

It is situated on ground comparatively flat, but is surrounded by mountains, or rather, hills; for the features of the country are here on a smaller scale.

The town, like all towns in Chile, is built on the usual plan. The streets are broad, and at right angles, and they are consequently parallel or perpendicular to each other. In the center of the town there is a plaza or great square, on one side of which is a rude sort of abode called the governor's house, where a number of dirty-looking soldiers without shoes, and with little on them but a poncho, are seen sitting under a corredor, or lying about asleep.

I rode up to the guard, and asked a man who had an old sword in his hand, where la fonda was. He settled the point very quickly by saying, "No hay fonda"; however, I learned that there was a house where travelers were occasionally received, and he directed me to it. When I got there, I found it locked up. I knocked at the door for some time in vain; at last, a woman from the opposite side of the street told me that the people were gone away, and that the house was empty.

It was summer, and the sun, which in Chile is always burning, was to us who had come down from the snow so exceedingly overpowering that I found it necessary to get into the shade somewhere or other, so I told my story to the women, and asked them where we could get shelter, a dinner, or even anything to drink. They said that the woman at the corner pulpería (shop) sold lemonade; but, as I was setting off, I saw at a little distance a quantity of rich clover-grass which had just been cut, so I filled my arms with it, and walked towards my mule. The grass was delightfully green, and the smell quite refreshing. The mule pricked up his long ears as he saw me coming; I threw it down before him, and took the iron mameluke bit out of his mouth. After eating some mouthfuls of it, he began to look about him, and I have seldom felt more provoked than I was to see him walk away from it, and in preference begin to eat some hot, dry, dirty straw, which was lying on a dungheap.

We then went to the shop, and I asked the old woman what in the world we were to do—that we had come out of the Andes, were going next morning to Santiago, or, as they term it, to Chile, and that we wanted food and lodging for the night. She told me that the only thing to be done was to hire a room, and then get a person to cook whatever we wanted.

This sounded hopeless, but I soon found that we had no alternative; so leaving my companion to drink a glass of lemonade, and to take a siesta in the old woman's bed, I went out on foot, following a little boy without shoes, and was at last led to the door of one of the largest houses in the place. The boy went inside, and in a short time he returned with a large key in his hand, followed by a well-dressed elderly lady, who asked me to walk in. I declined, and went with the boy some distance down the street; at last he stopped at a door, unlocked it, and we entered a room full of feathers and fleas, and without any glass in the window. "Aquí está," said the boy, and he added that I was to pay two reals (ten pence) a day. He said I could get dinner cooked at the next house. I accordingly went there, and found a woman who had the remains of very great beauty, and her daughter, of about eighteen years of age, who very much resembled her.

They both received me with the greatest kindness, and they insisted on my lying down on the bed. The old lady asked me what I would have for dinner for my party, and I told her all we wanted was the very best dinner she could give us, and that I begged to leave it to her good taste and judgment.

Away she went to get all the materiel, while her daughter attended to me. She brought me a plate of the most delicious cool figs I ever tasted, and then a glass of iced lemonade, and all the time I was eating the figs she was sitting by the bedside pitying me.

In about two or three hours the party arrived, mules and men quite fagged and exhausted, and I spoke to the capataz about starting early in the morning. He lived about two leagues from the town, and by agreement was to provide us with fresh mules for the baggage, and horses for ourselves; but I could see he was not inclined to be off early, so I insisted on his bringing the mules and horses that evening. He said that they would have nothing to eat, so I gave him two dollars to buy grass, and off he went, promising that he would be back in the evening.

I had just time to bathe, when our dinner was ready; and as the young woman brought us dish after dish, the party observed, first, that she was the most interesting looking girl they had ever seen, and secondly, that they had never eaten a dinner so well dressed; but the same delirium which, on coming from the snow of the Andes, had made them "babble o' green fields," caused them to err in their judgments on other parts of creation; and really, when we returned from the plain to Villa Nueva, our dinner was badly cooked, and the poor young woman was only said to be "rather pretty!"

The evening arrived, but not the capataz or his mules, and we did not know where to send for him; but an hour before daybreak the peon came to say that the capataz had turned him away; that he had spent the two dollars I had given him in drinking with his wife; that he had not given us the proper quantity of spare mules at Mendoza, and he begged us to take him before the governor.

The sun was already up, when the capataz arrived. He had brought several of the poor tired mules, fresh mules for the riders, and a broken-kneed horse for me; but he was himself mounted on a fine prancing horse. I took his horse from him, put my saddle upon it, and desiring my party to take him before the governor, galloped off towards Santiago.

The road soon became very bad, as the path ascends a cuesta, which it is necessary to climb and to descend by zigzags; however, as soon as I got on level ground by myself I galloped along, and it was quite delightful to be thus reminded of the pace of the pampas, after having crawled along so many days on the back of a mule.

I soon got to the house at which we had agreed to sleep, and which is about halfway between Villa Nueva and Santiago. It is a pulpería, and was filled with peons drinking; however, they had got bread and wine, and I sent a man off to get a sheep; there was also a nice stream of water for bathing. In the course of three or four hours, several of the party arrived on horses, and they were in high spirits at the triumph they had gained over the capataz. They said that the governor had heard their cause, and had then ordered them to give the capataz a hundred lashes, but that as they did not exactly know how or where they were to inflict this punishment, they begged him to have the goodness to change it; upon which the governor said, that if I preferred it, I might pay him only six dollars for each of his mules, instead of eight, which was the sum agreed for. The latter award was certainly the best of the two; and, accordingly, when the capataz arrived, I assured him that if he had behaved well I should have given him, in addition to his agreement, the usual *gratificación*; but, for his cruelty to his mules, I should most certainly inflict upon him one of the punishments to which the governor had sentenced him; and I left him for some time, uncertain which of the two he was to receive.

We all slept in the yard of the pulpería, on the ground, and long before daybreak we started. I galloped on by myself, and at first took the wrong path; but as soon as I found by my compass that it was leading me away from Santiago, I changed my course, and at last came to a fire, round which a family were sleeping. After the usual barking of the dogs was silenced, I was directed where to go, and I crossed a number of small hills, until I came to the large uncultivated plain of Santiago. I was more than two hours galloping across this plain, which, from want of irrigation, produces no sort of herbage, but only scattered shrubs.

When I got within two leagues of the city, I came to

water, and then the road was occasionally a pontano through which, not knowing the passes, I had great difficulty to wade. An English horse would certainly have stuck in it, but those of the country, being accustomed to it, walk through very slowly, extricating their legs with the greatest caution.

X

SANTIAGO

I was now met by, and I overtook, men, women, boys, priests, &c. on horseback, either coming from or going into town, all at a canter, and in very singular dresses. Many of the horses were carrying double, sometimes two giggling girls, sometimes a boy with his grandmother behind him; sometimes three children were cantering along upon one horse, and sometimes two elderly ladies; then a solitary priest with a broad-brimmed white hat and white serge petticoats tucked up all about him, his rosary dangling on his mule's neck, and his pale fat cheeks shaking from the trot. Milk, and strawberries, and watermelons were all at a canter, and several people were carrying fish into the town tied to their stirrups. Their pace, however, was altogether inferior to that of the pampas, and the canter, instead of the gallop, gave the scene a great appearance of indolence.

The spurs of the peons were bad, and their stirrups the most heavy, awkward things imaginable. They were cut out of solid wood, and were altogether different from the neat little triangle which just holds the great toe of the gaucho of the pampas.

On crossing the bridge, which is at the entrance of the town, the market was underneath me, on some low ground on the left. A number of people were selling fruit, vegetables, fish, &c., which were lying on the ground, and as the sun was now oppressively hot, each parcel was shaded by a small canvas blind, which was fixed perpendicularly into the ground.

As I rode along the streets I thought they looked very mean and dirty. Most of the houses had been cracked by earthquakes; the spires, crosses, and weathercocks, upon the tops of the churches and convents, were tottering, and

out of the perpendicular; and the very names of the
streets, and the stories, "Aquí se vende, &c.," which are
over all the shops, were written as crooked and irregular
as if they had been inscribed during an earthquake. They
were generally begun with large letters, but the man had
apparently got so eager about the subject that he was often
obliged to conclude in characters so small that one could
hardly read them, and in some places the author had
thoughtlessly arrived at the end of his board before he had
come to the end of his story.

The great plaza has a fountain in the middle, and the
Director's palace on one side. This building looks dirty
and insufficient; it is of a fantastic style of architecture,
and its outline is singular rather than elegant: part of it is
used as a guardroom. The soldiers were badly dressed;
some were blacks, wearing gold earrings, some were
brown, and some of a mongrel breed.

It was just eight o'clock as I rode across this square.
The bell of one of the churches tolled, and every individual, whether on horseback or on foot, stopped; the men all
pulled off their hats, the women knelt down, and several
people called to me to stop. The guard at the palace
presented arms, and then the soldiers crossed themselves;
in about ten seconds we all proceeded on our respective
ways. This ceremony is always repeated three times a day,
at eight in the morning, at noon, and at eight in the evening. I inquired my way to the English hotel, and found
there a hard-working, industrious Englishwoman, who
was the landlady. She told me she had not "an inch" of
room in her whole house, which was filled with what she
termed "mining gentlemen." I asked her where I could
go; she said she could not tell, but she offered to send one
of her servants with me to a "North American lady," who
sometimes took in strangers. I went accordingly, and was
introduced into a room which had a mat, a few highly
varnished, tawdry, wooden chairs, and a huge overgrown
pianoforte. One side of the room was glazed like a green-
house, and looked into another small room. Two long,

thin, vulgar-looking girls, who talked through their noses, now came in, and told me a long story about "mama," the object of which was, that mama was coming, and accordingly in she came. They were all at once asking me to be seated, and were inquiring into my history, when I informed the lady, that I had called to inquire whether she had accommodation in her house for strangers. Oh yes, she had a very nice room which she could let to me; there was no bed in it, but she could lend me chairs. I asked to see it; to my horror and astonishment, she led me to the glazed side of her room, and opening the glass door, she told me that was the room. I had a great deal of very troublesome business on my mind, and all I required for the very few days I was to be at Santiago was a little quietness and solitude. "Good heavens!" said I to myself, as I looked out of this wretched lanthorn, "how could I wash or make myself at all comfortable, either in body or mind, in such a place as this? Those girls, and that terrible pianoforte, would be the death of me! I am afraid, madam," addressing myself to the old lady, "this will not exactly do," and then out of the room, and out of the house, I walked.

I went back to the Englishwoman, who was very civil. The sun was burning me to pieces, I was quite exhausted, and I begged her to let me lay down anywhere in the shade, for that I had ridden almost all night, and was tired. She replied that she had positively no place. I told her I had been sleeping on the ground for many months, and that she surely had some little corner in which I might go to sleep. She said, "Nothing but the carpenter's shop." "Oh!" I said, with delight, "that will do famously"; so she led me to the place, and in a few seconds I was fast asleep among the shavings.

In three or four hours my party arrived, and the landlady had by this time hired two empty rooms for them, and afterwards one small one for me. She got me a table, with two chairs, and she told us we could breakfast and dine with all her guests. This was not a very agreeable arrangement, but furnished lodgings are not to be had at Santiago, and I had therefore no alternative than that of hiring an empty house, and then getting furniture and servants; but to clean the former, and break in the latter were occupations which I had no wish to undertake, particularly as I was going so shortly to inspect mines in different directions.

I had several letters, which at Buenos Aires I had been requested to take to Santiago, and these I at once delivered to a person to whom I was addressed. I had a drawing very carefully rolled up and sealed, which I had been told at Buenos Aires was the picture of a child in England, for his mother at Santiago. The lady happened to live close to the house to which I had taken my letters; and as I thought the picture of her child would be very acceptable, I called and delivered it to her myself. She was in one of the best houses in the town, and was surrounded by a very nice family of all ages. While I was talking to her she opened and unrolled the paper, and after glancing at it for a moment, she passed it to her family, who looked at it one after another with an apathy which quite provoked me. It was then handed to me, and I no sooner saw what it was than I bowed to the family, and left in the hands of the lady, not a picture of her child, but a schoolboy's large, coarse chalk drawing of the head of John the Baptist!

During the short time I was at Santiago, I was constantly occupied in gaining information, without which I could not have commenced my inspection of the mines; and as many unforeseen difficulties were impeding my progress, and occupying my attention, I had neither time nor inclination to enter into any sort of society, or to see any more of Santiago than what chanced to be going on in the streets.

The town is full of priests—the people are consequently indolent and immoral; and I certainly never saw more sad examples of the effects of bad education, or a state of society more deplorable. The streets are crowded with a set of lazy, indolent, bloated monks and priests, with their heads shaved in different ways, wearing enormous flat hats, and dressed, some in white serge cowls and gowns, and others in black. (I was one day in a hairdresser's shop at Santiago, when a priest came in to have his head shaved, and I stopped to see the operation. The priest was a sleek fat man of about forty, with a remarkably short nose and a sallow complexion. The man lathered him with the greatest respect, and then shaved the lower part of his head about an inch above his ears all round, and discovered bumps which a student of Gall and Spurzheim would have been shocked at. His head was as deadly white as young pork; and while the barber was turning the priest's head in different directions, I really thought it altogether the most uncivilized operation I had ever witnessed; and when it was finished, and the man stood up, he looked so very grotesque that I could scarcely refrain from laughing.)

The men all touch their hats to these drones, who are also to be seen in the houses, leaning over the backs of their chairs, and talking to women who are evidently of the most abandoned class of society. The number of people of this description at Santiago is quite extraordinary. The lower rooms of the most reputable houses are invariably let to them, and it is really shocking beyond description to see them sitting at their doors, with a candle in the back part of the room burning before sacred pictures and images.

The power of the priests has diminshed very much since the Revolution. They are not respected; they have almost all families, and lead most disreputable lives. Still the hold they have upon society is quite surprising. The common people laugh at their immorality, yet they go to them for images and pictures, and they send their wives and daughters to confess to them. Three times a day the people in the streets take off their hats, or fall down on their knees. Every quarter of an hour during the night the watchman of each street sings as loud as he is able a prayer of "Ave María purísima," and then chants the hour and a description of the night.

During the day one constantly meets a calash drawn by two mules, driven by a dirty boy in a poncho, and followed by a line of inhabitants with their hats off, each carrying a lighted candle in a lantern; every individual in the streets kneels, and those who have windows towards the streets (who are generally the females I have described) are obliged to appear with a lighted candle. In the inside of the carriage sits a priest, with his hands uplifted and clasped. In this system of depravity the great sinner pardons the little one. Sins are put into one scale and money into the other and, intent upon the balance, both parties forget the beauty and simplicity of the religion which they nominally profess.

The siesta at Santiago is as long as it is at Mendoza. The shops are shut at noon, and remain closed for four or five hours, during which time all business is at an end.

The climate of Santiago is similar to that of all the parts of Chile which I visited. The day in summer is burning hot; the nights delightfully cool. During the day, the sun, reflected from the mountains which surround the town on every side, and which, of course, obstruct the breeze, has a greater heat than is natural to the latitude. At night the cold air rolls down the snowy sides of the Andes, and fills the Chilean valleys with a cool atmosphere, which is unknown to the great plains on the other side of the cordillera. The effect of this stream of cold air is very agreeable, and people, whose occupations screen them from the sun in the day, enjoy their evening's ramble; and as the sky is very clear, the climate of Chile is often described as being extremely healthy. Yet the least learned, but perhaps the most satisfactory proof of the healthiness of a climate is not the brightness of the stars, or the color of the moon, but the appearance of men's and women's faces; and certainly the people of Chile in general, and of Santiago in particular, have not a healthy appearance. The English there, also, look very pale and

exhausted, and although they keep each other in countenance, it appeared to me that a strong dose of British
wind, with snow and rain, and a few of what the Scotch
call "sour mornings," would do them a great deal of good.

CONVENT

Group of people on the outside whispering and speaking
through the keyhole, the hinges and the cracks of the door
—turnabout filled with old linen—door half-opened by a
janitress to take in two large models on wheels, the one of
a brown cow, the other of a brown bull—door of the
chapel open—chapel divided into two parts by a double
grating, one of iron, the other of wood; the lattices about
the size of those in a cottage window. At one end the altar
glittering with silver, mummery, and candles; at the other
side of the grating the nuns assembled at vespers—some
were sitting at the sides and back of the chapel—others
kneeling in the middle, even close to the grating, and with
their faces towards the altar. They appeared to be almost
all very old, fat women, short and thick—complexions
stained with garlic and oil, and countenances soured by
long confinement. They were praying as if they were sick
and tired of it, and as if they neither cared nor knew what
they were saying. Four or five were playing on fiddles,
which they held up to their necks like men—one was
sawing an immense double bass, and another was blowing
with a large hand bellows into the lungs of a little organ,
on which a sister-nun was playing. They all sang together,
and I never heard sounds less melodious. Age had taken
all softness from their voices, and had left nothing but a
noise which was harsh, squeaking, and discordant. The
women were old and ugly, and the scene altogether was
saddening. Their dresses consisted of white caps and large
black gowns—their hair was concealed, and their features
were so hard that it was difficult to say whether they were
old men or old women—the serge gown concealed their
figures—figures which were intended as the ornaments of

creation. When one fancied the lives they might have led
—the assistance they might have afforded to society—the
friendships they might have enjoyed, and the pleasing
natural duties they might have performed, it was melancholy to see them lost to the world, and only occupied in
screaming in Latin through iron bars to candles and pictures.

On my right there was a young monk, who remained
on a bench close to the wall all the time I was there. He
was confessing a nun through some holes in a plate of tin,
which was let into the convent wall which separated them;
and since the days of Pyramus and Thisbe, there can never
have been a more regular flirtation. The monk was much
more anxious to talk than to hear, and I could not help
smiling when I saw him with great eagerness of countenance putting sometimes his mouth, and sometimes his
ear, to the tin plate. However, when I turned towards the
group of old nuns who were before me, I felt that it
mattered but little to society whether they were confessing
their old sins, or planning new ones; but it was distressing
to think that the young and the innocent, who were rising
in the world, were still the victims of such a mistaken
custom—for surely nothing can tend to blunt the good
feelings of the young more than the reflection that even
their thoughts of yesterday are already recorded by a man;
and if an evil genius wished to prepare a man who should
be peculiarly unfitted for so delicate a confidence, what
could he do better than doom him to idleness and celibacy,
deny him children of his own, and feed him upon oil and
garlic?

XI

THE GOLD MINES OF
EL BRONCE DE PETORCA

At about two o'clock in the morning we got up, and before
we had eaten our breakfast, the mules arrived with two
peons. There were two mules for each person, and they
were all driven loose into the yard. "Come now! Vamos!"
said one of the Cornish miners, who was always cheerful
and ready to start, upon which the party all got their
bridles and went down into the yard. The capataz took
my bridle and promised to give me a good beast, and I
stood for a few moments looking down upon the group
from the large corredor or balcony. Each man was choos-
ing his own mule; and as, from sad experience, he had
learned the difference between riding a good mule and a
bad one, it was a point of some consequence. It was amusing to see each individual trying to look an animal in the
face, to guess his character by the light of the moon, while
the cunning creature, aware of his intention, was constantly hiding his head among his comrades, and turning
his heels towards every person who approached him. As
soon as the mules were saddled, which was always a
troublesome and dangerous operation, we mounted, and
rode out of the yard, followed by the loose mules, who
trotted after the madrina, or bell mare, which was driven
on by one of the peons.

As we passed through the streets the watchmen were
singing the hour, with the usual hymn of "Ave María
purísima"; and it was quite singular to hear their different
ways of chanting it.

Our road passed across the plain of Santiago, and
although we cantered, it was nearly three hours before we
got to the mountains, and then for the whole day we had
either to climb up one side of a barren mountain, or to
scramble down the other. These mountains, from want of

rain, afford scarcely any pasture. The soil upon them is cracked in a most singular manner, and the fissures are so deep and frequent that it is apparently dangerous to ride over them.

After traveling until our mules were quite tired, we arrived, after the sun had set, at a small hamlet of mud huts. There had been a church, but the great earthquake of 1822 had converted it into a heap of ruins. The scene in the village was a very gay one. It was Christmas, and the usual festivities were going on. There were two or three rooms built of boughs and filled with young women and gauchos, who were dancing to the music of a guitar. On our arrival we had been led to the hut of a man who was the richest in the village; and as soon as we had taken our saddles into his house, we went out to join the dance. The sight of a few unexpected strangers added to the cheerfulness of the scene; the guitar instantly sounded louder, and the people danced with greater vigor. Round the room were rough poles as benches, on which sat the ladies who had danced; their partners were seated on the ground at their feet, and their earnest attentions cannot exactly be described. We were received with great hospitality, and in two minutes I saw my party all happy, seated on the ground, and as completely *enfants de famille*, as if they had been born there.

After remaining with them a short time, I returned to the hut. I found the master very sulky; he had turned all our saddles out of his house, and for some little time he would not speak to me. However, I insisted that he should point with his finger where the saddles were, and accordingly I found them on the ground, outside a little hut, in which was one of the miners cooking our supper. We had slept so long in the open air that it was of little consequence. I must do this man the justice to say that though he was naturally a sulky fellow, he had intended to do right. He wished to have done the honors of his hut to strangers, and he accordingly gave the Cornish miner some eggs, but the man, intending to pay for them, honest-

ly told him there were not half enough, which the landlord considered as a breach of politeness.

While I was sitting on a horse's head, writing by the
blaze of the fire, I saw two girls dressing for the ball. They
were standing near a stream of water, which was running
at the back of the hut. After washing their faces, they put
on their gowns, and then twisting up their hair in a very
simple pretty way, they picked, by the light of the moon,
some yellow flowers which were growing near them. These
they put fresh into their hair, and when this simple toilette
was completed, they looked as interesting, and as nicely
dressed, as if "the carriage was to have called for them at
eleven o'clock"; and in a few minutes, when I returned to
the ball, I was happy to see them each with a partner.

In the morning, before day, we started, and for many
a league my companions were riding together, and dis-
cussing the merits of their partners. The country we rode
over was mountainous, and it was very fatiguing both to
mules and riders. I had just climbed up a very steep part
of the mountain, and, with one of my party, was winding
my mule through some stunted trees, when I suddenly met
a large-headed young man, of about eighteen years of age,
riding his horse at a walk, and with tears running, one
after another, down his face. I stopped, and asked him
what was the matter, but he made no reply. I then asked
him how many leagues it was to Petorca, but he continued
crying, and at last he said, "He had lost . . . ." "Who have
you lost?" said I, debating whether it was his mother or
his mistress. The fellow burst into a flood of tears, and
said, "Mis espuelas" (my spurs), and on he proceeded.
One cannot say much for the lad's fortitude, yet the loss of
spurs to a gaucho is a very serious misfortune. They are in
fact his only property—the wings upon which he flies for
food or amusement.

The sun was getting low, and the mules quite tired
with the rocky barren path on which they had toiled,
when we came to the top of a mountain, from which we
suddenly looked down upon the valley of Aconcagua,

which is a long narrow plain, irrigated by a fine stream of water. The contrast was quite extraordinary—the color of the trees and grass was black rather than green, and vegetation so rank and luxuriant that the huts literally appeared smothered in the crops around them. This picture is one which is constantly met with in Chile; and as the produce of these plains, when irrigated, is greater than that of any of the world, Chile has often been called one of the richest countries. But although these productive spots deservedly attracted the attention of the Spaniards, who found that the necessaries of life were there so easily obtained, yet the country is generally so mountainous, and so large a proportion of it is incapable of irrigation, that its population must hereafter be infinitely less than that of the pampas, although at present it very much exceeds it.

On getting into the small town of Aconcagua, the church of which is in ruins, and almost every house cracked by earthquakes, we found the same sort of festivities which we had joined the evening before, but they were less interesting, because they were more formal. The plaza was covered with sheds, in which were people dancing, and when we rode up to the fonda, we saw the yard filled with people, sitting in bowers made of branches of trees, with others dancing or drinking.

We were eating our dinner at a small table in the yard when a person came up and offered us a room at his house, and in the evening he came to take us to it. When he unlocked the door, which was on the ground floor, we found the room filled with sacks of Indian corn, hides, rubbish of all sorts, and swarming with fleas. However, we made room, and slept there, and in the morning, after thanking the man for his lodging, we breakfasted at the fonda, where we might have slept much better.

Early the next morning we started on our fresh horses and mules, leaving the tired ones in a potrero, and visited a silver mine which was within a league of the town. We then pursued our course over barren mountains, and at about twelve o'clock in the day we reached the village of

Petorca, which consists of one long principal street, with other short ones at right angles. The church, like that at Aconcagua, was overturned by the earthquake of 1822, and the walls of the houses were cracked and rent from top to bottom.

I had a letter of introduction to the principal person, who was extremely polite, and was very anxious that we should spend the evening with him. However, I at last prevailed upon him to get us fresh mules, and about two o'clock, after we had had some refreshment, we set off with him to visit some trapiches and mills which had existed before the earthquake. We found the roofs shaken from two of the huts, and the rest tottering. The two mills were so completely annihilated that it was difficult to trace the foundation on which they had stood, and the water was diverted from its course.

In the evening our landlord gave us a most excellent supper, and the following morning, an hour before sunrise, we started to inspect the gold mines of El Bronce de Petorca, which were six miles from the village, and about a hundred and sixty from Santiago.

I visited this mine accompanied by a very intelligent Chilean miner, who with several of his comrades was in a mine on this lode a hundred fathoms deep when the great earthquake of the 19th of November 1822, which almost destroyed Valparaiso, took place. He told me that several of his comrades were killed, and that nothing could equal the horror of their situation. He said that the mountain shook so that he could scarcely ascend; large pieces of the lode were falling down, and every instant they expected the walls of the lode would come together, and either crush them or shut them up in a prison from which no human power could liberate them. He added, that when he got to the mouth of the mine the scene was very little better; there was such a dust that he could not see his hand before him. Large masses of rock were rolling down the side of the mountain on which he stood, and he heard them coming and rushing past him without being able to see how to avoid them, and he therefore stood his ground, afraid to move. In almost all the mines which we visited in Chile we witnessed the awful effects of these earthquakes, and it was astonishing to observe how severely the mountains had been shaken.

We got back to Petorca by ten o'clock, and as our host said he could give us fresh mules, I sent ours quietly on, and we agreed to start as soon as we had had a couple of hours' sleep.

After taking leave of our kind host, and bowing to the ladies, who were all standing at their doors, I went to the mule which had been provided for me, and saw by the wrinkles in his nose that he had some mischief in his head. However, he stood perfectly still, and allowed me to put my foot into the stirrup; but as soon as I threw my leg over him he jumped sideways about a yard; my heel went on to the top of some baggage which was upon the back of another mule, and my long gaucho's spur got entangled in it. The mule, seeing that his plot had succeeded, began to kick, and with one leg up in the air, it was quite impossible to keep my seat. I fell on my head, and was stunned by the fall; however, as soon as I recovered I remounted him, expecting that he would kick again—*au contraire*, he was perfectly satisfied with what he had done, and he proceeded as quietly as a lamb.

XII

THE GOLD MINE OF CAREN
AND THE SILVER MINE
OF SAN PEDRO NOLASCO

After inspecting the old holes which had been worked on the lode, and gazing with great interest at the Pacific, which was apparently hanging in the air beneath us, we descended the side of the rock, sometimes upon hands and knees, for about three hundred and fifty feet, until we came to the hut where we had slept. The situation of this hut was singularly perilous. The path which ascended to it from the plain was so steep that in riding up we constantly expected to tumble backwards over the tails of our mules; and when we got near the hut, the muleteers declared that it was altogether impossible to proceed, and this was so evident that we dismounted and scrambled over the loose stones until we got to the hut.

The mine had not been worked for a hundred years, but it was now for sale. The hut had been just built, and a couple of miners ordered to live in it. A small space had been scarped out for the foundation of the hut, which was so close to the precipice that there was not room to walk round it. Above it, on the mountain, were loose rocks, which by the first earthquake would probably be precipitated. Beneath was the valley, but at such a depth that objects in it were imperfectly distinguished. I consulted with the two mining captains, and we all agreed that the plain was about three thousand feet beneath us; but this only gives our imperfect idea of it, and is probably altogether incorrect; for although I spent some months among the Andes, I was always deceived in the distances, and found that my eye was altogether unable to estimate proportions to which it had never been accustomed—a trifling but a very striking proof of which occurred at this hut.

We were sitting with the native miners when one of

my men called out that there was a condor, and we all instantly ran out. He had been attracted by the smell of a dead lamb, which we had brought with us, and which was placed upon the roof of the hut. The enormous bird, with the feathers of his wings stretched out like radii or fingers, majestically descended without the least fear, until apparently he was only ten or fifteen yards above us. One of the men fired at him with a gun loaded with large shot—his legs fell, and he evidently had received the whole of the charge in his chest; yet he instantly bent his course towards the snowy mountains which were opposite to us, and boldly attempted to cross the valley; but, after flying for many seconds, he could go no further, and he began to tower. He rose perpendicularly to a great height, and then, suddenly dying in the air—so that we really saw his last convulsive struggle—he fell like a stone.

To my astonishment, he struck the side of the mountain apparently close to us; and as I looked at him lying on the rock, I could not account for his being so very near us (apparently thirty or forty yards), for as he had evidently fallen perpendicularly, the distance which separated us was of course the hypotenuse of a right-angled triangle, the base of which it had taken him many seconds to fly.

I sent one of the Chilean miners, who were accustomed to descend the mountain, to fetch him, and I went into the hut, and remained eight or ten minutes. On coming out, and asking for the bird, I was surprised to see that the man was not halfway to him; and although he descended and ascended very actively, his return was equally long. The fact was, that the bird had reached the ground a great distance from us; but this distance was so small in proportion to the stupendous objects around us, that, accustomed to their dimensions, we were unable to appreciate it.

As soon as we returned to Santiago from the gold mine of Caren, we ordered fresh mules; and the next morning,

before daybreak, we set off to inspect the silver mine of
San Pedro Nolasco, which is in the Andes, about seventy-
five miles southwest from Santiago. For a few miles we
traversed the plain of Santiago, which was cool and refreshed by the night air. Just as the day was dawning we
reached the foot of the mountains, and then following the
course of a large rapid torrent, we continued for several
hours on the east side of it, climbing along a path which
appeared to overhang the water.

As the sun gradually rose, the mountains on the opposite side were scorched by the heat, while we for several
hours were in the shade and cool; but the line of shadow,
after crossing the torrent, gradually approached us, the
sun at last looked over the high mountains which were
above us, and that instant commenced the fatigue of the
day.

The valley of Maipú, down which the stream descended, is one celebrated in Chile for its beauty. Bounded
on both sides by the barren mountains of the cordillera,
this delightful vale winds its course on both sides of the
river or torrent of Maipú; and although it is uncultivated,
yet it is ornamented with a great variety of shrubs and
fruit trees.

For several leagues we passed trees loaded with ripe
cherries, and peach trees which were bending towards
the ground with the weight of their crop. The ground
underneath was covered with the peach stones of the last
year's produce, and there must be thousands of these trees
whose fruit has never once been tasted by man. The
ground, although it produced shrubs and trees, had no
appearance of pasture, which cannot in a hot climate exist
without irrigation.

After traveling about thirty miles, we crossed the
torrent of Maipú, on a suspension bridge of hide ropes,
the construction of which I examined with great attention,
as I was surprised to find it exactly similar to those which
I have seen constructed in England of iron, although this
bridge has been there beyond the memory of man. The

path across it was covered with hurdles, and as the torrent was much swollen, the water was rushing over it with great velocity, which, of course, made the bridge incline very much. Our mules were unwilling to cross it, and I certainly should have thought it dangerous, had not a man who was on the opposite side beckoned to us to come over. The bridge bent with the weight of the mules, and the water rushed with great violence against them, but they leaned against it, and we all passed it without accident; and in returning rode over it in the dark.

After continuing our journey about four miles, we came to a small establishment for reducing the ores raised from San Pedro Nolasco, and for the interesting process of amalgamation, and we remained here for the evening to inspect it.

Without entering into a description of the establishment, it will only be observed that the works were laid out with a great deal of ingenuity, with a very happy regard to economy, and that, although they of course did not possess many of the mechanical advantages which a large capital might have afforded them, yet they were on a plan suited to the resources of the country, and upon the whole were well adapted for the economical reduction and amalgamation of ores upon a small scale.

The next morning, before sunrise, we continued our course towards San Pedro Nolasco, and for four or five hours followed the course of the river. The valley became narrower, and as we proceeded the trees and shrubs became smaller and more stunted—around us on every side were the Andes covered with snow. Our path was in many places very dangerous, being infinitely more so than any of the parts we had crossed in coming from Mendoza over the cordillera. The laderas were literally only a few inches wide, and were covered with stones, which were so loose, that every instant they rolled from under the mules' feet, and fell with an accelerating violence into the torrent. As I rode almost the whole of the day by myself, I would willingly have got off; but the mules will never lead, and besides this, when once a person is on the ladera, on the back of his mule, it is impossible to dismount, for there is no room to get off, and the attempt to do so might throw the mule off his balance and precipitate him into the torrent, which was at an extraordinary depth beneath. In some few places, the path was actually washed away, and the mule had only to hurry over the inclined surface the best way he could; but the manner in which these patient animals preserve their footing is quite extraordinary, and to know their value one must see them in the cordillera. After passing two or three very violent torrents, which rushed from the mountains above us into the river beneath us, we came to one which looked worse than those which we had with great difficulty crossed; however, we had no alternative but to cross it, or return to Santiago. We attempted to drive the loose mules across, but one had scarcely put his feet into it, when he was carried away, and in less than twenty yards the box which he had on his back was dashed to pieces, and its contents were hurried down the surface of the stream. In order to get across, we put a lasso round our bodies, and then rode through; but the holes were so deep, that the water occasionally came over the neck of the mule, and we passed with great difficulty. These poor creatures are dreadfully afraid of crossing these torrents; it is only constant spurring that obliges them to attempt it, and sometimes in the middle of the stream they will refuse to advance for several seconds. When the water is very deep, the arrieros always tie the lasso round their bodies; but I never could conceive it was any security, because if the torrent will dash a wooden box to pieces, a man's skull would surely have a very bad chance. I was, therefore, always very glad when I found myself across them; and, as our lives were insured in London for a large sum of money, I used often to think, that if the insurers could have looked down upon us, the sight of the laderas and of these torrents would have given a quickness to their pulse, a flush to their cheek, and a singing in their ears, very unlike the symptoms of placid calculation.

Shortly after passing this torrent, we turned towards the south, and began to climb the mountain of San Pedro Nolasco, which I can only describe by saying that it is the steepest ascent which we ever made in all our expeditions among the Andes. For five hours we were continually holding on by the ears or neck of our mule, and the path was in some places so steep that for a considerable time it was quite impossible to stop. We soon passed the limits of vegetation. The path went in zigzags, although it was scarcely perceptible, and if the mules above us had fallen, they would certainly have rolled down upon us, and carried us with them.

In mounting we constantly inquired of the arriero if the point above our heads was the summit, but as soon as we attained it, we found that we had still higher to go. On both sides of us we now came to groups of little wooden crosses, which were the spots where people formerly employed in the mine had been overtaken by a storm, and had perished. However, we continued our course; and at last, gaining the summit, we found ourselves close to the silver lode of San Pedro Nolasco, which is situated on one of the loftiest pinnacles of the Andes. A small solitary hut was before us, and we were accosted by two or three wretched-looking miners, whose pale countenances and exhausted frames seemed to assimilate with the scene around them. The view from the eminence on which we stood was magnificent—it was sublime; but it was, at the same time, so terrific, that one could hardly help shuddering.

Although it was midsummer, the snow where we stood was, according to the statement made to me by the agent of the mine, from twenty to a hundred and twenty feet deep, but blown by the wind into the most irregular forms, while in some places the black rock was visible. Beneath was the river and valley of Maipú, fed by a number of tributary streams, which we could see descending like small silver threads down the different ravines. We appeared to have a bird's-eye view of the great chain of the Andes, and we looked down upon a series of pinnacles of indescribable shapes and forms, all covered with an eternal snow. The whole scene around us in every direction was devoid of vegetation, and was a picture of desolation, on a scale of magnificence which made it peculiarly awful; and the knowledge that this vast mass of snow, so cheerless in appearance, was created for the use, and comfort, and happiness, and even luxury of man; that it was the inexhaustible reservoir from which the plains were supplied with water—made us feel that there is no spot in creation which man should term barren, though there are many which nature never intended for his residence. A large cloud of smoke was issuing from one of the pinnacles, which is the great volcano of San Francisco; and the silver lode, which was before us, seemed to run into the center of the crater.

As it was in the middle of the summer, I could not help reflecting what a dreadful abode this must be in winter, and I inquired of our guide and of the miners concerning its climate in that season. They at first silently pointed to the crosses, which, in groups of three and two and four, were to be seen in every direction; and they then told me, that although the mine is altogether inaccessible for seven months in winter, yet that the mineers used to be kept there all the year. They said that the cold was intense, but that what the miners most dreaded were the merciless temporales, or storms of snow, which came on so suddenly that many miners had been overtaken by them, and had perished when not a hundred and fifty yards from the hut. With these monuments before my eyes, it was really painful to consider what the feelings of those wretched creatures must have been when, groping about for their habitation, they found the violence of the storm unabating and irresistible. It was really melancholy to trace, or to fancy I could trace, by the different groups of crosses, the fate of the different individuals. Friends had huddled together, and had thus died on the road; others had strayed from the path, and from the scattered crosses, they had apparently died as they were searching for it. One group was really in a very singular situation; during a winter particularly severe, the miners' provisions, which consist of little else than hung beef, were gradually failing, when a party volunteered, to save themselves and the rest, that they would endeavor to get over the snow into the valley of Maipú, and return if possible with food. They had scarcely left the hut, when a storm came on, and they perished. The crosses are exactly where the bodies were found; they were all off the road; two had died close together, one was about ten yards off, and one had climbed to the top of a large loose fragment of rock, evidently to look for the hut on the road. The view from San Pedro Nolasco, taking it all together, is certainly the most dreadful scene which in my life I have ever witnessed; and it appeared so little adapted or intended for a human residence, that when I commenced my inspection of the lode, and of the several mines, I could not help feeling that I was going against nature, and that no sentiment but that of avarice could approve of establishing a number of fellow creatures in a spot which was a subject of astonishment to me how it ever was discovered.

As the snow was in many places fifty feet deep on the lode, I could only walk on the surface from one boca-mina to another; but when I had done this, I took off my clothes, and went down the mine which it was my particular object to inspect. All the rest had long ago been deserted, but in this one there were a few miners, lately sent there, who were carrying on the works on the old system which had been exercised by the Spaniards, and to which these men have all their lives been accustomed.

At first we descended by an inclined gallery or level, and then clambered down the notched sticks, which are used in all the mines in South America as ladders. After descending about two hundred and fifty feet, walking occasionally along levels where the snow and mud were above our ankles, we came to the place where the men were working. It was astonishing to see the strength with which they plied their weighty hammers, and the unremitted exertion with which they worked; and strange as it may appear, we all agreed that we had never seen Englishmen possess such strength, and work so hard. While the barreteros, or miners, were working the lode, the acarreadores were carrying the ore upon their backs; and after we had made the necessary observations, and had collected proper specimens, we ascended, with several of these acarreadores above and below us.

The fatigue of climbing up the notched sticks was so great that we were almost exhausted, while the men behind us (with a long stick in one hand, in the cloven end of which there was a candle) were urging us not to stop them. The leading acarreador whistled whenever he came to certain spots, and then the whole party rested for a few seconds. It was really very interesting, in looking above and below, to see these poor creatures, each lighted by his candle, and climbing up the notched stick with such a load upon his back, though I occasionally was a little afraid lest one of those above me might tumble, in which case we should have all preceded him in his fall.

We were quite exhausted when we came to the mouth of the mine; one of my party almost fainted, and as the sun had long ago set, the air was so bleak and freezing—we were so heated—and the scene was so cheerless, that we were glad to hurry into the hut, and to sit upon the ground round a dish of meat, which had long been ready for us. We had some brandy and sugar, and we soon refreshed ourselves, and I then sent out for one of the acarreadores with his load. I put it on the ground, and endeavored to rise with it, but could not, and when two or three of my party put it on my shoulders I was barely able to walk under it. The English miner who was with us was one of the strongest men of all the Cornish party, yet he was scarcely able to walk with it, and two of our party who attempted to support it were altogether unable, and exclaimed "that it would break their backs."

The load which we tried was one of specimens which I had paid the acarreador to bring up for me, and which weighed more than usual, but not much, and he had carried it up with me, and was above me during the whole of the ascent.

While we were at one end of the hut, drinking brandy and water, seated upon our saddles, and lighted by a brown tallow candle which was stuck into a bottle, and which was not three yards from a hide filled with gunpowder, the few miners we had seen at work had been relieved by others who were to work through the night. They came into the hut, and without taking the least notice of us, prepared their supper, which was a very simple operation. The men took their candles out of the cloven sticks, and in the cleft they put a piece of dried beef; this they warmed for a few seconds, over the embers which were burning on the ground, and they then ate it, and afterwards drank some melted snow water out of a cow's horn.

Their meal being over, they then enjoyed the only blessing fortune had allotted to them, which was rest from their labor. They said nothing to each other; but as they sat upon the sheepskin, which was the only bed they had, some fixed their eyes upon the embers, while others seemed to ruminate upon other objects.

I gave them what brandy I had, and asked them if they had no spirits, to which they gave me the usual answer, that miners are never allowed to have spirits, and with this law they seemed to be perfectly satisfied.

When one contrasted their situation with the independent life of the gaucho, it was surprising that they should voluntarily continue a life of such hardship.

XIII

FROM SANTIAGO TO MENDOZA

December 31st, Santiago, midnight.—Mules arrived for us to recross the cordillera to return to Buenos Aires—a large drove—two mules for each person—spare ones for the baggage. At one o'clock in the morning the mules were laden and ready—went across the street to the fonda, to get some breakfast, which was laid for us at one end of a long table—at the other end were two Scotchmen sitting without their coats, waistcoats, or neckcloths—(midsummer).

They had been drinking in the new year—in their heads there was "mair brandy than brains," yet their hearts were still true to their "auld respected mither." The room was evidently moving round them—they were singing (with action) "Auld Lang Syne," and the one that was pitted with the smallpox seemed to feel it as much as the other; they held out glasses to us, and begged us to join them—we declined—amusing contrast between them and the gravity of my party, drinking tea, with their pistols in their belts, and prepared for a long journey—full chorus of "Rule Britannia," then "God Save the King"; shook hands with the two Scotchmen—drank half a glass of their brandy, and then mounting our mules—we groped along in the dark towards the black mountains of the cordillera.

Got to Uspallata late in the evening with two of the party; at sunset the rest arrived. Mules tired—the maestro de posta had three horses, and being anxious to get on to Mendoza (ninety miles), three of us rode all night. We had three times traveled the road, and therefore went by ourselves. About halfway we saw a fire on the ground, and by the blaze we perceived some person near it—rode up to light our cigars, called several times, but found no one.

On arriving at the hut near Villavicencio we mentioned the circumstance, and were told it was probably an Englishman who had passed the hut that day on foot!—that he had probably been afraid of us, and had concealed himself, or had run away.

Rested, and then got fresh horses at Villavicencio. The sun was most dreadfully hot. We galloped across the plain—forty-five miles—each at our best pace—proceeded straggling, like the wounded Curiatii. I got into Mendoza three hours before the second—he got in two hours before the third, whose horse was tired on the road.

In riding along the plain I passed a dead horse, about which were forty or fifty condors; many of them were gorged and unable to fly; several were standing on the ground devouring the carcass—the rest hovering above it. I rode within twenty yards of them; one of the largest of the birds was standing with one foot on the ground and the other on the horse's body—display of muscular strength as he lifted the flesh and tore off great pieces, sometimes shaking his head and pulling with his beak, and sometimes pushing with his leg. (The manner in which the gauchos catch these birds is to kill a horse and skin him; and they say that, although not a condor is to be seen, the smell instantly attracts them. When I was at one of the mines in Chile, I idly mentioned to a person that I should like to have a condor. Some days afterwards a gaucho arrived at Santiago from this person with three large ones. They had all been caught in this manner, and had been hung over a horse; two had died of galloping, but the other was alive. I gave the gaucho a dollar, who immediately left me to consider what I could do with three such enormous birds.)

Got to Mendoza, and went to bed. Wakened by one of my party who arrived; he told me that seeing the condors hovering in the air, and knowing that several of them would be gorged, he had also ridden up to the dead horse, and that as one of these enormous birds flew about fifty yards off, and was unable to go any farther, he rode up to him, and then, jumping off his horse, seized him by the neck. The contest was extraordinary, and the ren-contre unexpected. No two animals can well be imagined less likely to meet than a Cornish miner and a condor, and few could have calculated, a year ago, when the one was hovering high above the snowy pinnacles of the cor-dillera, and the other many fathoms beneath the surface of the ground in Cornwall, that they would ever meet to wrestle and "hug" upon the wide desert plain of Villa-vicencio. My companion said he had never had such a battle in his life; that he put his knee upon the bird's breast, and tried with all his strength to twist his neck; but that the condor, objecting to this, struggled violently, and that also, as several others were flying over his head, he ex-pected they would attack him. He said that at last he succeeded in killing his antagonist, and with great pride he showed me the large feathers from his wings; but when the third horseman came in, he told us he had found the condor in the path, but not quite dead.

XIV

Again the Pampas

In the evening some of the miners strolled with their guns, and procured us a supper of roasted parrots. We found these birds in great numbers from the Atlantic to the Pacific, living together in flocks. They are seldom silent, and when they assemble on trees, they bend down their heads, flap their wings with a sort of thrilling motion, and with no one to call them to order, they all, young and old, chatter at once with more good humor than harmony. The plumage of their breasts is always of the most gaudy and brilliant description, but their backs are invariably of the color of the country they inhabit. In the region of wood, the bark of which is generally green, and bright yellow, they are of those hues — in the plain of grass, their backs are a mixture of brown and green, and they so resemble the surface of the country that, as they skim over it, it is as difficult to trace them as the partridge when flying over ploughed land; but as soon as they get close to a person riding, they suddenly give a wild scream, in one second they all turn, and when the sun suddenly shines on their gaudy bosoms, the flash is extraordinary and beautiful.

I waited some time at the post hut, talking with the old lady, who was always very kind and glad to see me, and was also extremely clever and entertaining; I then mounted my horse, and, after galloping nearly an hour, I overtook the coach just as it had reached the banks of the river Desaguadero, which was unusually deep and rapid. There was nothing but a small bark, but we lost no time in filling it with the luggage, and then made preparations for dragging the carriage through the river. I took off my clothes, and throwing them into the boat, I tied a silk handkerchief round my neck, and put my watch there to keep it dry. I had my pistols in my right hand, and I then rode into the river. The horse was instantly out of his depth, but he swam over very well. Just as I had scrambled up the bank, a man, dressed in a dirty-looking poncho, who lived in a hut about a hundred yards off, came up and asked to be paid for the boat; I told him I would pay him as soon as the coach was over, and I asked him to take care of my pistols for me, and he accordingly took them to his hut.

We then set to work to get the carriage over, which was a very curious operation. The bank to descend to the river was much steeper than 45°, and it was therefore necessary to fix a peon, with his horse and lasso to the back part of the carriage, to prevent its oversetting; we had also lassos fastened as guys on each side. Two or three peons fixed their lassos to the end of the pole, and one swam across the river with a long dragrope, to which eight or ten horses were affixed to assist in dragging the carriage. As soon as these arrangements were made, the carriage was lowered down the bank, but its weight was so great that it dragged after it the peon and horse fixed to retain it; and while our party also were hauling at the rope, it was curious to see them all dragged down the bank. As soon as the carriage came into the river, although the wheels and perch were unusually high, it was nearly filled with water. In this state the peons whose lassos were fixed to the end of the pole, with all the horses at the dragrope, dragged the carriage slowly along the bottom of the river: however, when it was about halfway across, it would come no farther, and the horses which were on the steep bank had little power to draw. The carriage remained in this hopeless and singular situation more than an hour, during which time we were occupied in altering the dragropes, and arranging them more advantageously.

I found the sun so burning hot that several times I swam about on my horse to cool myself, and then galloped on the opposite side of the river, and I cannot express the

delightful feeling of freedom and independence which one
enjoys in galloping without clothes on a horse without a
saddle.

When the horses and peons were ready, they all
started together, and at last the carriage began again to
move; and the peons then spurring, flogging, and cheering
their horses, it was dragged up the bank.

While they were putting the luggage into the wet
carriage, I dressed myself, and then rode up to the hut to
pay the man for his boat. He demanded twelve dollars,
which I knew was too much, and I therefore refused to
give it. In a moment, he was in a violent passion; he
addressed himself sometimes to me, and sometimes to
some gauchos who were sitting drinking; and he was approaching me with menacing gestures, when I took my
pistols off his table, and before I placed them into my belt,
I put the muzzle of one of them against his front tooth,
and told him very quietly that I would pay him what was
proper, but that if he demanded more, I would only pay
him with that pistol. In an instant, the man desired one of
the gauchos to saddle him a horse, in order to ride to the
governor of San Luis, who he said was a relation of his, and
he then told me that he was himself a judge. I laughed at
him, and telling him that he was a bad judge in his own
cause, I left him, and rode after the coach.

In about half an hour the fellow overtook me, and
without speaking he galloped by me. He was dressed in his
judicial robes; that is, he had on a coarse blue jacket, with
scarlet cuffs and collar, and a long saber. I now continued
my course for the remainder of this post, which is fifty-one
miles, changing my horse when I overtook the droves of
loose horses which preceded the carriage.

This stage is really one of the most singular examples
of South American traveling which I have witnessed. We
started with seventy horses, which were driven before us
at a gallop. These horses were all loose; and the country
hot sand, covered with trees and brushwood. The trees are
principally the algarroba; they were about the size and

shape of apple trees, and were sufficiently high to hide the horses. This drove of wild loose animals was driven by a man and a boy, and it was quite surprising, as I galloped along the road, to see these fellows constantly darting across the path before me, in close pursuit of the horses, which were never to be seen in the road. In the plains of grass it is even wonderful to see how the troops of horses are driven on, but in a wood it is much more astonishing; and it is a beautiful display of horsemanship to see the gauchos galloping at full speed among the trees, sometimes hanging over one side of their horse, and sometimes crouching upon his neck to avoid the branches of the trees. The carriage road is a space cleared of large trees, but it is often covered with bushes, which bend under the carriage in a most extraordinary manner.

I arrived at the post some hours before the carriage, and had supper ready by the time it arrived. This post is only one stage from San Luis; the postmaster is the brother of the governor of the province, and he was at San Luis when I arrived, but his capataz asked me, with great seriousness of countenance, whether I was the person who had galloped after the judge at the Desaguadero, in order to shoot him. He told me that the said juez had just passed, and had taken a fresh horse to get to San Luis before I arrived there. We slept that night at the post, or rather on the ground before it; and it was curious, in the morning, to see the different groups of people, who had also slept there, dressing themselves—men, women, and children were all sitting up as if just risen from the grave. Some were scratching themselves, some were rubbing their eyes, some puting on their hide sandals. The hens were pecking about them, particularly round the table at which we had supped. The great dogs, who had also just awakened, were walking very slowly with their tails between their legs towards the corral, where there is always a supply of food for them. The infants were still sleeping, each upon a lamb's skin, on the ground, without a pillow, covered only with a piece of dirty blanket, and sometimes the hens would perch upon them. As soon as the horses were caught, we set off, and I galloped into San Luis, and got there an hour before the carriage. I found the post as usual; there was nothing to be had—no fruit, though in the middle of summer, and no milk. The people of the post house told me that the juez had arrived there last night, and it appeared that his story had been much inflamed by his gallop. As soon as the carriage arrived, the juez and an ordenanza, or horse soldier, came up to the post, and told me that I was to come immediately to the governor. I had a white linen jacket on, which was really too dirty to go in, so I resolved to put on a coat. On opening my portmanteau, out came a quantity of water, and I found that it had been filled in passing the Desaguadero—my coat was consequently dripping wet; however, I put it on, and as I knew the way, I galloped towards the barracks, followed by the juez and the ordenanza. I found the square filled by a set of most wretched-looking persons, who were assembled to be sent to Buenos Aires to fight against the Portuguese. There were about three hundred of them, and the night before they had endeavored to gain their liberty, and had tried to overpower their guard. They were covered with old ponchos, but had very little on besides; they seemed to have been badly fed, and were altogether the wildest-looking crew I ever beheld.

The governor was standing in the middle of the square, surrounded by a number of officers, and I dismounted and walked up to him. He began, very hastily, by telling me the juez's story; however, I asked him if he would allow me to tell mine. I told him that it was so much my duty to respect governors and governments that if I had known the man who was before us had been in his employment, I would have respected him, though his conduct did not deserve it; but that instead of wearing the clothes he now had on, he was dressed in a dirty poncho—was drinking aguardiente with the gauchos, and that I had therefore no idea he was a judge. I explained the circumstances, and the governor then told the man that he had asked too much, and that I was to pay him three dollars less than he had demanded. The governor offered, very obligingly, to lend me the money as I had no change; he paid the man, who had not a word to say, and who had his ride, one hundred and eighty miles, for nothing. I then went into the governor's room, and mentioned to him that our carriage wanted a trifling repair, but that the blacksmith had told me he could not work at it without permission from him, as he was employed in making chains to take the three hundred recruits down to Buenos Aires. The governor very politely sent for the smith, and desired him to work for me for three hours; after which I made my bow, and then galloped to the post.

While the smith was repairing the carriage, I looked again at the town of San Luis. Each house in the town has a large garden, in which there is nothing but what they cannot prevent from growing, such as fig trees, vines, peach trees. The walls of their gardens are often towards the streets, which gives the place so little the appearance of a town, that the first time I came to San Luis, I actually asked a man how far I was from el pueblo; to which he replied that I was in it. From twelve till four or five every day, the whole population of the town is asleep, and when the people awake, they have no other idea than that of satisfying their hunger, by eating the old dish, carne de vaca. Far from having any luxuries, they have not even what we term common necessaries; and it seems incredible that there should be no individual in the whole town, or indeed the province, who even professes to know anything of medicine or surgery; and that there is no shop at which one can purchase the simplest medicines. If a person is ill, he dies or recovers as it may happen, but he has no assistance. If he dislocates or breaks a bone, his friends may regret the accident, but he has no help. The gaucho, who lives in his little hut on the pampas, must necessarily be without medical assistance, and it is interesting to see his young family living so completely under the sole protection of Providence; but for the capital of a province to continue in such a state, shows an indolence which its peculiar situation can only excuse.

The post house of San Luis is also in a state which would scarcely be credited. It is in nothing better than the post huts of the pampas; it has no window, the door cannot be shut, and it is more filthy than can well be described. It was late before the carriage was ready; however, as I was anxious it should get on, it started with three changes of horses, about an hour before sunset, to go to the next post, which is thirty-six miles. I rode by a different road, and it was settled that we should all get on by moonlight; however, as soon as the sun set the weather began to look wild, and it became very cloudy and dark. I continued to gallop until I could not see my hand before me, and as I knew there were many holes and vizcacheras, we then slackened to an ambling canter. It is really very nervous, disagreeable work even to canter over a strange country when it is quite dark; however, I was anxious if possible to reach the post, as it was the nearest hut we could get to. I was cantering along, expecting every moment to tumble head over heels, when my horse suddenly struck his chest against the back of the gaucho's horse, which was standing still. As soon as I found out what it was I spoke to the man, but I received no answer; I then called out, when he told me from some distance that he was feeling with his hands for the path—that he could not find it—and that there were so many holes that, as we had lost ourselves, it would be dangerous to proceed. I accordingly dismounted, and, unsaddling my horse, I had instantly my bed ready. I could see nothing, but the gaucho and I made our beds side by side, and as soon as we lay down, he tied the horses' bridles round his own neck, and he then was asleep in a moment.

The country we were in was much infested by salteadores, but as I was always well-armed, I felt quite secure, and in a short time I was also asleep. About midnight I was awakened by the rolling of thunder, and, sitting up, I saw by the occasional flashes of lightning that

I was lying on brown coarse grass, and that there were here and there a few shrubs. Some large heavy drops of rain began now to fall, and I made up my mind that we were to have a drenching shower; however, it was useless to move, for I did not know where to go, so I took the usual precaution, which is to place the skin which, in dry weather, one lies on, over my head, and I then went to sleep. Before the day began to dawn I was awakened by the gaucho, who told me the horses were lost. I told him very sulkily to go and look for them, and, with my head under the skin, I again dropped off to sleep. I was awoke by the heat of the sun, and jumping up found that it was above the horizon, and that it was late. I looked earnestly round me, but, except a few shrubs, there was nothing but "the wind blowing and the grass growing"—in every direction was a vast expanse of plain. I began to think that the man had returned to San Luis, and I really did not know what I should do. The sun was oppressively hot, and I was standing in despair, gazing at the recado which had formed my bed, when I heard the distant notes of a Spanish song behind me, and turning round I saw the gaucho galloping towards me, and driving my horse before him. In a few moments he came up; my horse was of course without a bridle; the fellow had played me the old trick of hiding it, and declaring it was lost. However, I was glad to get my horse upon any terms, and I cut a piece of hide, which served to guide him, and we then galloped towards the post, from which we were distant about thirteen miles.

I there got some breakfast, while they were catching another horse for me. They had neither bread nor milk, but I got some water, a couple of eggs, and an old woman warmed some charqui for me over the embers. I was surrounded by several women and girls, all three-quarters naked, who asked me if I could give them maté or sugar, "por remedio." As soon as my horse was saddled, I purchased the bridle of the gaucho who had stolen mine, and then galloped on. The country, which from Mendoza is covered with wood, now changes to the long brown and yellow grass, which, excepting a few straggling trees, is the sole produce of the remainder of the province of San Luis, and of the two adjoining provinces of Córdoba and Santa Fe. In the whole of this immense region there is not a weed to be seen. The coarse grass is its sole produce; and in the summer when it is high, it is beautiful to see the effect which the wind has in passing over this wild expanse of waving grass; the shades between the brown and yellow are beautiful—the scene is placid beyond description—no habitation nor human being is to be seen, unless occasionally the wild and picturesque outline of the gaucho on the horizon—his scarlet poncho streaming horizontally behind him, his balls flying round his head, and as he bends forward towards his prey, his horse straining every nerve; before him is the ostrich he is pursuing, the distance between them gradually diminishing—his neck stretched out, and striding over the ground in the most magnificent style—but the latter is soon lost in the distance, and the gaucho's horse is often below the horizon, while his head shows that the chase is not yet decided. This pursuit is really attended with considerable danger, for the ground is always undermined by the vizcachas, and the gaucho often falls at full speed. If he breaks a limb, his horse probably gallops away, and there he is left in the long grass, until one of his comrades or children come to his assistance; but if they are unsuccessful in their search, he has nothing left but to look up to heaven, and while he lives drive from his bed the wild eagles, who are always ready to attack any fallen animal. The country has no striking features, but it possesses, like all the works of nature, ten thousand beauties. It has also the grandeur and magnificence of space, and I found that the oftener I crossed it, the more charms I discovered in it.

On approaching the huts, it is interesting to see the little gauchos, who, brought up without wants, and taught to consider the heaven over their heads as a canopy under which they may all sleep, literally climb up the tails of the horses which they are unable otherwise to mount, and then sport and gallop after each other, while their father's stirrups are dangling below their naked feet. In the foreground of nature, there is perhaps no figure so beautiful as that of a child who rides well, and the picturesque dress of the little gauchos adds very much to their appearance. I have often admired them as they have been sent with me from one post to another. Although the shape of their body is concealed by the poncho, yet the manner in which it partakes of the motion of the horse is particularly elegant. It is interesting, too, to see the heedless, careless way in which these little chubby-faced creatures ride, and how thoughtlessly they drive their horses among vizcacheras, which would break in with the weight of a man.

When I got to El Morro, I resolved to wait there for the carriage, for I had the keys of my portmanteau, and both I and my party wanted money. El Morro consists of a few mud huts, as usual without windows; and as I stood at the door of the post room no human being was to be seen, except occasionally a woman with her hand or poncho shading off the sun from her head as she crossed the broad irregular street which divided the huts from each other. Here and there a horse was seen tied to the outside of a hut, and a little tame ostrich was before the door running after flies. The atmosphere was quivering with the heat, and resounding with the shrill cry of millions of flies enjoying the sun. There were no trees to be seen, and neither fruit nor flowers to be had. I went to the woman of the post to ask what she had to eat: "Nada (nothing), señor," she replied. I asked for several things which, from seeing a church and a small congregation of huts, I thought might have been procured, but I received the usual answer, "No hay," and I was obliged to send out for a live sheep. I then took a siesta, and it was late in the evening before the carriage and the party arrived. They had stopped at a hut a few leagues from San Luis, and had afterwards broken the pole of the carriage, which had delayed them several hours. After supper I thought that the weather looked very wild, and I therefore got into the

four-wheeled carriage to sleep, and one of the party was
close to me in the two-wheeled one. The nine peons were
scattered about the ground. Two of our party slept under
the carriage, and the rest on the ground in different places.
About midnight we were awakened by a most sudden and
violent whirlwind, which blew several of the party's
clothes away, and they were afterwards found in the river.
There was so much dust that we could scarcely breathe,
and all was utter darkness until the lightning suddenly
flashed over our heads. The thunder was unusually loud,
and down came a deluge of rain. The wind, which was what
is termed a pampero, was now a dreadful hurricane, and I
expected every moment that it would overturn the carriage. I sat up and looked around me, and in my life I
never saw so much of the sublime and of the ridiculous
mixed together. While the elements were raging, and the
thunder was cracking and roaring immediately above us,
the lightning would for an instant change the darkness to
the light of day. In these flashes I saw our party, who were
all hallooing one to another, in the most ludicrous situations. Some were lying in bed afraid to sit up, and holding
their ponchos and clothes, which were trying to escape
from them—some who had lost their clothes were running half-naked towards the post room—others had lost
their way, and were standing against a dead wall, not
knowing where to go. A French colonel, who had traveled
in the carriage from Mendoza, was lying on a stretcher
made of a bullock's hide, grasping his clothes, which were
now wet through, and vociferating at his cowardly servant,
who, instead of assisting him, was standing about ten
yards from him crossing himself. In vain did he call him in
Spanish every sort of "animal." The fellow, who had
literally been approaching his master, was riveted to the
ground by the unexpected sound of the church bell, which,
from the violence of the hurricane, occasionally gave a solitary toll. The rain beat so violently into the two-wheeled
carriage, and it shook so terribly, that its inmate could
bear it no longer, and ran through the rain. At last they all

got into the post room, and as I looked out of the window, I saw them all crowded together peeping over each other's heads at the door.

In the morning they found what they had lost, and the peons and the whole party looked very uncomfortable. Many of the peons had lain on the ground the whole time, and they were of course covered with the mud which had been formed by the dust and rain. The peons and the people told us they had never seen such a storm and pampero before in their lives.

The carriage was late in starting, and the sun was already up, when the French colonel and I agreed to make a call on the priest. He was dressed in a dirty white serge gown, tied round his body with a rope to whip himself with. He was really not more than four feet and a half high, and yet weighed more than any of our party; his neck was as thick as a bullock's, and he had not been shaved for several days. In his room, which had no window, were two or three old books, covered with dust, and a little crucifix affixed to the wall. I asked him if it was he who had tolled the bell during the storm; he said, Oh, no! that he had ridden a number of leagues the day before, and had slept so sound that he had not heard it, and had only just been informed of it

On account of the party's clothes being so wet, we lost a great deal of time, and it was seven o'clock before we started. The two carriages went by the road, but the post-master told a little gaucho to take me by a nearer cut. I followed this little child, who was not more than eight years old, for many leagues. He rode like the wind, and amused me extremely by a number of very entertaining stories which he told me. At last it began to rain, and the little boy said, "Quién sabe" if ever he should find out the post, for that he had never before come that way. It was no use stopping, and as I galloped along, I made the child tell me the directions which the postmaster had given to him, but I could make nothing at all of them. One would have thought by the child's description that it was a

mountainous country we were crossing, for he talked of
hills and valleys which I could not see; but the gauchos
do divide their plains into ups and downs, which no one
can distinguish but themselves. At last the child exclaimed,
that he could see a "cristiano" driving some horses, and
when we came to this man, he told us where the post was.

I found the horses at the post in the corral, and the
postmaster, whose house I had several times slept at, gave
me a horse with a galope largo (a long gallop), and a very
handsome gaucho as a guide. I had a long conversation
with this man as I galloped along, and I found him a very
noble-minded fellow. He was very desirous to hear about
the troops which the government of Mendoza had sent to
reinstate the governor of San Juan, who had just been
deposed by a revolution. The gaucho was very indignant
at this interference; and as we rode along, he explained to
me, with a great deal of fine action, what was evident
enough—that the province of San Juan was as free to elect
its governor as the province of Mendoza, and that Mendoza had no right to force upon San Juan a governor that
the people did not approve of. He then talked of the state
of San Luis; but to some question which I put to him, the
man replied, that he had never been at San Luis! "Good
heavens!" said I, with an astonishment which I could not
conceal—"have you never been to see San Luis?"—
"Never," he replied. I asked him where he was born; he
told me, in the hut close to the post; that he had never
gone beyond the plains through which we were riding, and
that he had never seen a town or a village. I asked him
how old he was: "Quién sabe," said he. It was no use
asking him any more questions; so, occasionally looking
at his particularly handsome figure and countenance, and
calling to mind the manly opinions he had expressed to me
on many subjects, I was thinking what people in England
would say of a man who could neither read nor write, nor
had ever seen three huts together, &c., &c., when the
gaucho pointed to the sky, and said, "See! there is a lion!"
I started from my reverie, and strained my eyes, but to

no purpose, until he showed me at last, very high in the air, a number of large vultures, which were hovering without moving; and he told me they were there because there was a lion devouring some carcass, and that he had driven them away from it. We shortly afterwards came to a place where there was a little blood on the road, and for a moment we stopped our horses to look at it; I observed, that perhaps some person had been murdered there; the gaucho said, "No," and pointing to some footmarks which were near the blood, he told me that some man had fallen, that he had broken his bridle, and that, while he was standing to mend it, the blood had evidently come from the horse's mouth. I observed, that perhaps it was the *man* who was hurt, upon which the gaucho said, "No," and pointing to some marks a few yards before him on the path, he said, "for see the horse set off at a gallop." (I often amused myself by learning from the gauchos to decipher the footmarks of the horses, and the study was very interesting. It is quite possible to determine from these marks whether the horses were loose, mounted, or laden with baggage; whether they were ridden by old men or by young ones, by children, or by foreigners unacquainted with the vizcacheras, &c., &c.)

The grass was shorter in this part of the province than it usually is, and it was very picturesque and curious as we went along to see bullocks' skulls lying in different directions. The skeleton of the bull's head was justly admitted by the ancients as an ornament in their architecture. In the pampas it is often seen lying on the ground bleached by the sun, with the horns upwards, and appearing as if the animal had just risen from his grave, and was moralizing to the living cattle which were feeding about him.

In consequence of what this man had told me respecting his birth, &c., I asked every one of the gauchos who rode with me from post to post, for the next six hundred miles, the same questions, and I found that the greater number of them had never seen a town, and that no one of them knew his age. When we came to the post,

which is one of the richest possessions in the pampas, I
found about twenty gauchos assembled to commence
breaking in the young horses, an operation which was to
be continued for many days. As the carriage was many
hours behind me, I resolved to see this, and, getting a fresh
horse, I rode immediately to the corral, and soon made
friends with the gauchos, who are always polite, and on
horseback possess many estimable qualities, which at the
door of their hut they appear to be devoid of. The corral
was quite full of horses, most of which were young ones,
about three and four years old. The capataz, mounted on
a strong steady horse, rode into the corral, and threw his
lasso over the neck of a young horse, and dragged him to
the gate. For some time he was very unwilling to leave his
comrades, but the moment he was forced out of the corral,
his first idea was to gallop away; however, the jerk of the
lasso checked him in a most effectual manner. The peons
now ran after him on foot, and threw the lasso over his
four legs, just above the fetlocks, and, twitching it, they
pulled his legs from under him so suddenly that I really
thought the fall he got had killed him. In an instant a
gaucho was seated upon his head, and with his long knife
in a few seconds he cut off the whole of the horse's mane,
while another cut the hair from the end of his tail. This,
they told me, is a mark that the horse has been once
mounted. They then put a piece of hide into his mouth, to
serve as a bit, and a strong hide halter on his head. The
gaucho, who was to mount, arranged his spurs, which were
unusually long and sharp, and while two men held the
animal by his ears, he put on the saddle, which he girthed
extremely tight. He then caught hold of the horse's ear,
and in an instant, vaulted into the saddle; upon which the
man, who was holding the horse by the halter, threw the
end of it to the rider, and from that moment no one
seemed to take any further notice of him. The horse instantly began to jump, in a manner which made it very
difficult for the rider to keep his seat, and quite different
from the kick or plunge of an English horse; however, the

gaucho's spurs soon set him going, and off he galloped, doing everything in his power to throw his rider. Another horse was immediately brought from the corral, and so quick was the operation, that twelve gauchos were mounted in a space which, I think, hardly exceeded an hour.

It was wonderful to see the different manner in which the different horses behaved. Some would actually scream while the gauchos were girthing the saddle upon their backs; some would instantly lie down and roll upon it; while some would stand without being held, their legs stiff, and in unnatural directions, their necks half-bent towards their tails, and looking vicious and obstinate; and I could not help thinking that I would not have mounted one of these for any reward that could be offered me, for they were invariably the most difficult to subdue.

It was now curious to look round and see the gauchos on the horizon in different directions, trying to bring their horses back to the corral, which is the most difficult part of their work, for the poor creatures had been so scared there that they are unwilling to return to the place. It was amusing to see the antics of the horses; they were jumping and dancing in different ways, while the right arms of the gauchos were seen flogging them. At last they brought the horses back, apparently completely subdued and broken in. The saddles and bridles were taken off, and the young horses immediately trotted towards the corral to join their companions, neighing one to the other. Another set were now brought out, and as the horses were kept out a very short time, I saw about forty of them mounted. As they returned to the corral it was interesting to see the great contrast which the loss of the mane and the end of the tail made between the horses which had commenced their career of servitude, and those which were still free.

The horses of the pampas are like the common description of Spanish horse, but rather stronger. They are of all colors, and a great number are piebald. When caught, they will always kick at any person who goes behind them; and it is often with great difficulty that they can be bridled and saddled. However, they are not vicious, and when properly broken in will allow the children to mount by climbing up their tails. In mounting, it is necessary to be very quick, and previous to dismounting, it is proper to throw the bridle over one side of the head, as the horses almost always run backwards if one attempts to hold them by the bridle when it is over the head, as in England.

Although I rode many thousand miles in South America, I was quite unable to learn how to select either a good horse or an easygoing one, for by their appearance I found it impossible to form a judgment; indeed, I generally selected for myself the worst looking horses, as I sometimes fancied that they went the best.

When first mounted, they often begin to kick and plunge, but by giving them a loose rein, and by spurring them, they will generally start, and when once at their pace, they go quiet. However, the kicking at starting is a most painful operation to undergo, for from hard riding the back and shoulders get so dreadfully stiff that such sudden and violent motion seems to dislocate the limbs.

The evening closed, but the carriages did not appear. I anxiously looked on the horizon for them, until it became dark; I then went into the post room, and ordered one of the women to bring me the roast beef and soup which was prepared for the party. I was quite ravenous, for I had been so occupied with the horses that I had forgotten that I had eaten nothing since daylight. The woman brought me a dirty sheet four times doubled, which she put on the little square table, then a bottle of wine; "Have you a glass?" "No hay, señor." "Oh, never mind," said I, putting the bottle to my mouth. The woman returned with the beef cut up into pieces, in a pewter dish; it was smoking, and looked very nice; and she also gave me some bread. I instantly took out of my pocket a clasp knife and fork. She asked me if I wanted anything else? "No," said I, putting a piece of the beef into my mouth; but as she was going out of the door, I called her back, and asked her to get me some salt. "Aquí está, señor," said the woman, apparently recollecting herself; and opening her right hand, she put very quietly upon the table some salt which she had intended for me, and because some of it stuck to her hand, she scratched it off with her fingers, and seemed resolved that I should have every particle of it.

There was no candlestick, but, with the beef, a little black girl about seven years old, and almost naked, brought in a crooked, brown, tallow candle, which she held in her hand all the time I dined. The little creature had gold earrings and a necklace of red beads. I gave her a large piece of bread, which she ate very slowly, with the most perfect gravity of countenance. As I was dining, I occasionally looked at her. Nothing was white but her eyes and the piece of bread in her mouth. She was watching every mouthful I ate, and her eyes accompanied my fork from the pewter dish to my mouth. With her left hand she was scratching her little woolly head, but nothing moved except her black fingers, and she stood as still as a bronze statue.

The carriage did not arrive, so I laid my saddle in front of the post, and slept there. It was late in the morning before one of the peons came to tell me that the two-wheeled carriage had broken down in spite of all its repairs; that it was in the middle of the plain, and that the party had been obliged to ride, and put the baggage on post horses, and that they would be with me immediately. As soon as they arrived, they told me their story, and asked what was to be done with the carriage. (After the party had left one of the posts about an hour, and when they were twelve or thirteen miles from it, they saw a man galloping after the carriage, endeavoring to overtake it. They stopped, and when he came up, they found it was the master of the post hut where they had slept. He said very civilly that they had forgotten to pay him for the eggs, and that they therefore owed him a medio [two pence half-penny]. They paid him the money, neither more nor less, and then galloped on, leaving the man apparently perfectly satisfied.)

It was not worth more than one hundred dollars; and it would have cost more than that sum to have guarded it, and to have sent a wheel to it six hundred miles from Buenos Aires; so I condemned it to remain where it was, to be plundered of its lining by the gauchos, and to be gazed at by the eagle and the gama—in short, I left it to its fate.

I had been much detained by the carriages, and I was so anxious to get to Buenos Aires without a moment's delay that I resolved instantly to ride on by myself. Three of my party expressed a wish to accompany me, instead of riding with the carriage; so after taking from the canvas bag sufficient money for the distance (about six hundred miles), I left the rest for the coach, and once more careless of wheels and axles, I galloped off with a feeling of independence which was quite delightful.

We traveled sixty miles that day, not losing one moment, but riding at once to the corral, and unsaddling and saddling our own horses. The next morning one of the party was unable to proceed, so he remained at the post, and we were off before daylight. After galloping forty-five miles, another said he was so jolted that he could not go on, and he also remained at the post to be picked up by the carriage. We then continued for sixteen miles, when the other knocked up, and he really was scarcely able to crawl into the post hut, where he remained. As I was very anxious to get to Buenos Aires, and was determined to get there as quick as my strength would allow, I rode sixty miles more that day, during which my horse fell twice with me, and I arrived at the post an hour after sunset, quite exhausted. I found nothing to eat, because the people who live at this post were bathing, so I went to another part of the river, and had a most refreshing bath. I then spread out my saddle on the ground, for the post room was full of fleas and vinchucas. The people had now returned from the river, and supper was preparing, when a young Scotch gentleman I had overtaken on the road, and who had ridden some stages with me, asked me to come and sing with the young ladies of the post, who he told me were very beautiful. I knew them very well, as I had passed several times, but I was much too tired to sing or dance. However, being fond of music, I moved my saddle and poncho very near the party, and as soon as I had eaten some meat I again lay down, and as the delightful fresh air blew over my face, I dropped off to sleep just as the niñas were singing very prettily one of the tristes of Peru, accompanied by a guitar. I had bribed the capataz to let some horses pass the night in the corral; we accordingly started before the sun was up, and galloping the whole day till half an hour after sunset, we rode a hundred and twenty-three miles. The summer's sun has a power which, to those who have not been exposed to it, is inconceivable, and whenever we stopped at the corral to get our horses, the heat was so great that it was almost insupportable. However, all the time we galloped, the rapid motion through the air formed a refreshing breeze. The horses were faint from the heat, and if it had not been for the sharp gaucho spurs that I wore I should not have got on. The horses in the pampas are always in good wind, but when the sun is hot, and the grass burnt up, they are weak, and being accustomed to follow their own inclinations, they then want to slacken their pace, or rather to stop altogether; for when mounted they have no pace between a hand gallop and a walk, and it is therefore often absolutely necessary to spur them on for nearly half the post, or else to stand still, an indulgence which, under a burning sun, the rider feels very little inclined to grant. As they are thus galloping along, urged by the spur, it is interesting to see the groups of wild horses which one passes. The mares, which are never ridden in South America, seem not to understand what makes the poor horse carry his head so low, and look so weary. The little innocent colts come running up to meet him, and then start away frightened; while the old horses, whose white marks on the flanks and backs betray their acquaintance with the spur and saddle, walk slowly away for some distance, and then breaking into a trot, as they seek their safety, snort and look behind them, first with one eye, then with the other, turning their nose from right to left, and carrying their long tails high in the air. As soon as the poor horse reaches the post he is often quite exhausted; he is as wet as if he had come out of a river, and his sides are often bleeding violently; but the life he leads is so healthy, his constitution is so perfectly sound, and his food is so simple, that he never has those inflammatory attacks which kill so many of our pampered horses in England. It certainly sounds cruel to spur a horse as violently as it is sometimes necessary to do in the pampas, and so in fact it is, yet there is something to be said in excuse for it; if he is worn out and exhausted, his rider also is—he is not goaded on for an idle purpose, but he is carrying a man on business, and for the service of man he was created. Supposing him to be ever so tired, still he has his liberty when he reaches the goal, and if he is cunning, a very long time may elapse before he is caught again; and in the meanwhile the whole country affords him food, liberty, health, and enjoyment; and the work he has occasionally performed, and the sufferings he has endured, may perhaps teach him to appreciate the wild plains in which he was born. He may have suffered occasionally from the spur, but how different is his life from that of the poor post horse in England, whose work increases with his food— who is daily led in blinkers to the collar, and who knows nothing of creation, but the dusty road on which he travels, and the rack and manger of a close-heated stable.

The country through which we rode this day was covered with locusts of a very beautiful color. They were walking along the road so thick that the ground was completely covered—some were hurrying one way and some another, but the two sets were on different sides of the road like people in the City of London. At one post these locusts were in such numbers that the poor woman, in despair, was sweeping them away with a broom, and they swarmed in crowds up my horse's legs. A little girl had given me some water, and I put my straw hat on the ground while I sat down to drink, and with feelings of very great pleasure I was looking at the mug; which was an English one, and on which was inscribed—

No power on Earth
Can make us rue,
If England to her-
Self proves true—

when I saw my hat literally covered with the locusts biting the straw. As soon as I took it up, these parti-colored creatures hopped off like harlequins. The number of them is quite incredible, and they would be a most serious enemy to any individual who should attempt to cultivate a solitary farm in the pampas—although a large population and general cultivation might perhaps keep them away.

We arrived late and very tired at the post, having ridden one hundred and twenty-three miles, and found the master Don Juan—— very busy, providing supper for a priest who had just arrived in a carriage. The water was extremely bad, and I began to think I should fare badly, when the priest asked me to partake of his supper, which was now smoking on the table. He had some good water in bottles, and we had a roasted lamb before us. The priest ate the heart, and seemed to enjoy his repast as much as I did. He was silent, but very kind, and occasionally nodded at the dish and said to me, "Come bien!" (Eat well.) After the lamb he brought out a box of sweetmeats, and he then put his hand up the large loose sleeve of his white serge gown and pulled out some cigars.

Next morning at daybreak we started. The French colonel's servant now began to complain, and after riding one hundred miles I saw no more of him, as he and the Scotch gentleman who had accompanied me stopped at sunset. I rode on about twenty miles, and the next day I rode one hundred and twenty miles, and reached Buenos Aires about two hours after sunset.

XV

GENERAL OBSERVATIONS
RESPECTING THE WORKING OF MINES
IN SOUTH AMERICA

When one reflects upon the immense riches which have proceeded from some mines, and the large sums of money which have been lost in others, it is evident that the inspection of a mine with a view of immediately working it with a large capital, is in any country an important and difficult duty. There are, perhaps, few subjects which require more deliberate and dispassionate consideration; for to be too sanguine, or to be too timid, are faults which it is easy to commit. In the former case, one builds upon hopes which are never to be realized; in the latter, one loses a prize which energy and enterprise might have secured; and the passions of the mind are never more eager to mislead the judgment than when the object to be considered is the acquisition of what are termed the "precious metals."

But if this is the case in civilized countries, where experience has recorded many valuable data, where the lode to be inspected may be compared with those which are flourishing and with those which have failed, where operations may be commenced with a cautious step, where the windlass may be succeeded by the whims, and the whims by the steam engine, how much more difficult is the task when the lode is in a foreign country, destitute of resources, experience, and population, and when as a stranger one is lead over a series of wild, barren mountains, to a desert spot, at once to determine whether the mine is to be accepted or not. As this has been my situation, I will venture to make a few imperfect observations on the subject.

The first object which draws the attention to a lode (which is a ramified crack or fissure in which ores with other substances are embedded) is its positive value or

contents, and this value has lately been estimated in England merely from the inspection and assay of a piece of the
ore; but of course this judgment is altogether erroneous,
for a large lode of a moderate assay may be more valuable
than a small lode of rich ores or assay, and an extraordinary rich lode may be too small to be worth the expense of working, while a very large poor lode may be
worked with profit.

But, besides these observations, the physical character of the lode must be considered; for the fissure is
seldom filled with ore, it contains also quartz, mundic (the
Cornish term for sulphurets of arsenic, iron, &c.), &c.,
&c. and is occasionally a strong box which contains no
riches at all.

It is therefore evident that besides the size of the lode,
and the assay, the average quantity of ore it contains is
also to be considered; because a large lode, with an occasional bunch (as it is termed) of rich ores, may not be so
worthy of working as a smaller lode with a number of
bunches of poorer ores. There is also another material
question—whether the lode is getting richer or poorer as
it dips? For a large lode, with rich assay, and frequent
bunches, but *diminishing* in value, may be calculated at
less value than a smaller lode with poorer assay, less frequent bunches, but *increasing* in value.

There are many other considerations, but the above,
perhaps, will satisfy those who have not reflected on the
subject, that the abstract value of a lode in *America* can in
no way be determined by the assay of a piece of ore in
England, particularly when it is known that specimens of
ores are often sent from South America as samples of lodes
from which they never were extracted. However, upon
the spot a calculation may be made of the probable produce of the mine; and in Cornwall, where the expenses of
the mine are known and certain, it is on this calculation
that almost all the *speculation* of the enterprise depends.
For the riches of lodes being subject to sudden variations,
they may increase or diminish in a surprising degree; still

the calculation rests in Cornwall upon as fair a basis as those which are made on the duration of human life, or the insurance of ships, &c., &c. But in South America the case is widely different; for besides the value of the produce of the mine, it is necessary to determine what will be the probable expense of working it, in order to weigh or compare the one with the other; and the absolute necessity of this, which is always done in mining, farming, and other speculations in England, is particularly obvious—for instance, in the provinces of Río de la Plata; for as one there rides over many hundred miles of rich land, which is unowned, and almost unknown, one cannot but reflect, that while, from want of population, industry, &c., such riches are lying on the *surface* unvalued, considerable difficulties would necessarily oppose the extraction of wealth from the bowels of the earth, by labor and machinery; and these difficulties, in many parts of the provinces, would be so great that it might satisfactorily be proved that the silver extracted from such mines would not be worth its weight in iron by the time it reached England; while the iron which was sent from England would cost more than its weight in silver by the time it reached the mine.

The following is a rough memorandum of some of the difficulties, physical, moral, and political, which would probably obstruct the working of mines in the provinces of Río de la Plata by an English association.

PHYSICAL

1. The great distances which separate the mines from their supplies of men, tools, materials, provisions, &c., and which separate one mine from another; badness of the roads; danger in passing the laderas; torrents and rivers without bridges, and often impassable; the locality of the mines, which are generally situated among lofty and barren mountains, without resources or supplies. The above would require expensive disbursements, and would often

cause a great delay, which, in mercantile operations, is a loss of money.

2. The dryness of the climate, which affords no water for machinery, or for washing the ores; but little even to drink; the mine itself dry, or nearly so. In consequence of the above, machinery is inapplicable, and the mines are better adapted to the limited exertions of a few people than to the extensive operations of an English association.

3. Heat of the climate; its effects on Europeans.

4. The desolate and unprotected plains between the mines and the port at which their produce would be shipped; the distance being, upon an average, more than a thousand miles of land carriage.

5. The poverty of the lodes, when compared with those of Mexico, Peru, or Potosí.

MORAL

The want of population—its effects. The general want of education, and consequently the narrow and interested views of the natives.—The richer class of people in the provinces unaccustomed to business.—The poorer class unwilling to work.—Both perfectly destitute of the idea of a contract, of punctuality, or of the value of time.— Among a few people the impossibility of obtaining open competition, or of preventing the monopoly of every article required, or the combination which would raise its price "ad libitum." The wild, plundering habits of the gauchos—the ready absolution of the priests—the insufficiency of the laws.

The want of experience, &c. in the Commissioner who has charge of the Association.—The character, constitution, habits, and expensive wants of the English and European workmen, ill adapted to the country.—The experience they have gained in Cornish copper mines inapplicable to the extraction of silver ores in South America. (See Memorandum A.) Europeans, overcome by the climate, become indolent from possessing large independent salaries in a country where wine and spirits are cheap

—women of the country—their characters.—Impossibility of the distant mines being frequently inspected, consequently the necessity of placing confidence, and of trusting gold and silver to individuals, many of whom in England would not be deemed persons of sufficient education for so difficult a situation. Probability that many would endeavor to perform their duty, but the certainty that one leak, whether from inattention or otherwise, would affect the interests of the whole.

POLITICAL

Important reasons why mines in South America, which formerly were worked with profit, would now ruin either Europeans or natives who should attempt to work them. (See Memorandum B.)

The instability and insufficiency of the national government of the United Provinces.—The provincial governments—their sudden revolutions.—The jealousy which exists between the provinces and Buenos Aires.—In spite of contracts, the governments would not allow large profits to go out of their provinces, or even to pass through them without contribution.—Individuals urged by the priests would overturn the governor—his acts and contracts fall with him.—The junta could voluntarily retire—their responsibility has then vanished—no remedy, and no appeal.

MEMORANDUM (A)

Those who propose to work a mine in Cornwall have the following advantages over those who propose with the same people to work a mine in South America:

1. In Cornwall, previous to commencing operations, they may inspect the mine themselves, and call any number of practical men to assist them. In South America they cannot do this, but must commit this important duty to one or more individuals.

2. In Cornwall, the lode is in a country whose climate

is favorable to great bodily exertion, and the general character of which is industry; but in South America the climate and excessive heat are unfavorable to great bodily exertion, and the general character of the country is indolence.

3. In Cornwall, the miners are subjected to a code of most admirable local regulations, which encourage competition and industry, and leave the idle to starve. In South America the miners are away from the force of all these regulations, and a high, fixed salary, with cheap wines and provisions, discourage competition and labor.

4. In Cornwall, although the miners have no theory, no schools, no books, yet, from long practice and experience, they most perfectly understand the geological construction of the country, the particular nature of the ores they seek, and the difficulties which they are likely to meet with. In South America, the geological construction of the Andes, and the mountains in which the mines are situated, is unknown to the Cornish miner—he is unacquainted with the ores he is to seek. The muriates, carbonates, pacos, colorados, and other nonresplendent ores, are by him so unnoticed, and undervalued, that the native miner has actually to point out to him the riches of the mine he has come to improve. (There exists in England a natural feeling of confidence in the exertions of English workmen, but I am afraid this expectation will not be realized in South America. The Cornish miner is, I believe, one of the best regulated workmen in England, but like all well-regulated workmen his attention has been directed to a particular object, and in proportion as he is intelligent upon that point he is ignorant of all others. By a division of labor, which is now so well understood in England, we have goldsmiths, silversmiths, tinsmiths, coppersmiths, whitesmiths, and blacksmiths, who are all ignorant of each other's trades; and if this is the case, why should a man whose life has been spent in working copper ores, be supposed able to search in any country for silver ores? There is certainly a much greater difference and

variety between the ores than there is between the metals.)

5. In Cornwall, the greatest difficulties are the subterraneous streams, which, in a humid climate and in a flat country, so influence the plan of operations that the art of mining in Cornwall is the art of draining, not on a general principle, but adapted to the geology of the country. In South America, as it never rains at Uspallata, and seldom rains in Chile, and as the winter showers, instead of sinking into the earth, rush down the precipitous sides of the mountains in which the lodes are situated, there is but little water; and therefore the Cornish plan of operations, and, consequently, the experience which the Cornish miner has gained, is inapplicable, for the difficulties which he has learned to overcome do not exist, while others oppose him which he has never been accustomed to meet.

6. In Cornwall, to drain the mines, steam engines can be procured at a short notice, and if, for any particular object, a large body of men are required for a few days, they can always be had; also whatever tools, wood, iron, rope, &c., may be required, can be obtained with a facility and punctuality known only in England. In South America, from the absence of water, the overpowering force of steam is unnecessary, inapplicable, and its great advantage is unattainable. In case of unforeseen difficulties requiring for a few days the assistance of a large body of extra laborers, it would be absolutely impossible to obtain them. Tools, iron, and materials could only be procured with the greatest possible difficulty. In many situations it would be necessary to send several hundred miles for materials. The purchaser would be assailed by every endeavor and combination to defraud. They would be delivered at a great expense of time and money; and in a country in which contracts are not understood, and time is of no value, there would be the most serious delays and disappointments.

7. In Cornwall, the expenses of the mine are known. The customary wages of the captains of the mines, the pay

of the miners who all work by tribute, or by tut-work, are accurately calculated. (Excepting the levels, which are always driven by tut-work [task work], the mines in Cornwall are all worked by tributers. These tributers are the common miners, who take their pitches by public auction, at which they agree to deliver the ore fit for market for different prices, from 6*d.* to 13*s.* 4*d.* in the pound, according to the nature of the ground, the ores, &c., &c. The adventurers of the mine, therefore, are tolerably sure of their profit before the work is begun, for the tributers pay the smith cost, candles, powder, breaking, wheeling, and drawing. They pay men for spalling and cobbing the large rocks, for separating the prill from the dradge, and they also pay girls for bucking the ores, and boys for jigging them.) The price of tools, iron, wood, rope, and all materials is known, and the sale of the ores by public auction gives an immediate and certain return. In South America the expenses of each mine can never be anticipated. The wages of the English captains and miners are very high; every article, if purchased a thousand times, would be the subject of a new bargain, and materials would be perhaps of double or treble cost, according to the people, and the spots from which they were to be obtained. After the extraction and reduction of the ores, the processes of smelting and amalgamation, which in Cornwall are unknown (the Cornish ores being always smelted in Wales), would be required.

8. In Cornwall, in case it should be deemed necessary to abandon the mine, the men can be discharged; the engines can be removed; the materials can be sold by auction, and the loss is only what has actually been spent on the mine. In South America, in case the mine should be deserted, to the sum sunk in the mine is to be added the expense of the men getting to the spot and returning, which in many cases would be very great; the construction of houses for officers and men, as also the establishments for smelting and amalgamation; the cost of engines and stores, which it would often be cheaper to abandon than to remove.

9. In Cornwall, the resources of a great mercantile country are so extensive, that public competition suppresses every sort of unjust combination, but among small communities of men this would be impossible; and without the slightest intention to blame any individual, I must declare, that from the Atlantic to the Pacific, I found that Englishmen and foreigners were preparing to monopolize every article that could be required for mining purposes; and that a large English capital, belonging sometimes to A., and sometimes to B., was considered by a pack of people as a headless, unprotected carcass, which was a fair subject for universal "worry."

MEMORANDUM (B)

Comparing the past and the present value of the mines in South America

On the discovery of the different countries of South America, the attention of the Spaniards was immediately directed towards the acquisition of those metals which all men are so desirous to obtain. Careless of the beauty of these interesting countries, their sole object was to reach the mines; and hence it is that the history of the American mines has always been considered the best history of the country. As soon as information was obtained from the Indians of the situation of the mines, however remote, small settlements were formed there; and with no other resources or supplies than those which nature had bestowed upon the country, they commenced their labors; they obtained their reward, and the arrival of the precious metals in Europe was hailed as the produce of intrepidity, industry, and science.

The mode, however, in which these riches were at first obtained, forms one of the most guilty pages in the moral history of man; and the cruelties which were exercised in the American mines are a blot on the escutcheon of human nature, which can never be effaced or concealed, and which is now only to be confessed with humility and contrition. Besides the mita, or forced labor of the Indians (the particular cruelty of which it is not the present object to describe), the whole system was one of extortion and oppression. (Those who formerly worked the South American mines have been accused of *ignorance*, in having brought ore and water from the mine on the backs of men. If the Indians employed had received English wages and English comforts, and had carried the small quantity which in England would be called a load, the *ignorance* of their masters would have been great indeed. But the case was very different. The Indian acarreadores were beasts of burden, who carried very nearly the load of a mule; and their food cost but little. Their unrecorded sufferings were beyond description; and I have been assured, from unquestionable authority, that, with the loads on their backs, many of them threw themselves down the mine, to end a life of misery and anguish.) The miners were barely sheltered from the weather; the use of all spirits was forbidden; their food was coarse, and the weighty tools which were placed in their hands were in themselves emblems of the ignorance, cruelty, and avarice of their masters.

However, there is no situation of misery or suffering to which the mind and body of man cannot be enured. The miner by degrees became accustomed to his labor and his tools; the slave, toiling under his load, ceased to complain; the cry of the sufferers became gradually silent, and in a short time no sound issued from the gloomy chamber of the mine but the occasional explosion of powder, the ringing blow of the hammer, and the faint whistle of the slaves, who thus informed the overseer that they had reached those points of the shafts at which, by law, they were allowed to rest.

The mine was said to have assumed a prosperous appearance, and men were talking aloud of the flourishing state of the South American colonies, and of the inexhaustible riches of the mines, when the spell was gradually broken. The revolution at last broke out, and, as if by magic, the miner found himself in the plain surrounded by his countrymen, marching forward in support of liberty, and lending his arm to exterminate from la patria the oppressors who were now trembling before them.

All the poor mines in South America from this moment were deserted, and the country was for many years in a state of warfare which it is not necessary to describe; but as soon as the victory was gained, and independence gradually established, one of the first acts to which many people had recourse was the working of the deserted mines, from which they naturally expected again to obtain wealth. Several of the miners had been killed in the wars, and others, wearing the spurs and poncho of the gaucho, enjoyed a life of wild and unrestrained liberty. There were some, however, who voluntarily returned to the profession in which they had been trained, and were willing again to embrace a life whose hardships had become habitual; but the forced labor of the Indian was now wanting; and although this system of cruelty had been long abolished in many parts of South America, yet its existence in some places, and the unjust encouragement which the Spaniards had given to mining, in exclusion of every other branch of industry, had, up to the period of the Revolution, greatly assisted the working of the mines.

Operations were, however, recommenced at almost all the old mines. They were all tried; but, generally speaking, they were all abandoned, because they did not pay. With little inquiry into the cause, the reason assigned was the want of intelligence and capital; and people, frustrated in this object, and incapable of contending with the difficulties which impeded any step towards civilization in the insulated, remote, and almost impracticable situations in which they often found themselves, yielded to the habits of indolence in which they still exist.

If the above rough and imperfect description of the mines of South America is deemed correct in its general features, it will account for a phenomenon which, in visiting several deserted mines, I was for a long time totally unable to comprehend.

In many places we found lodes worked to considerable depths, but the lode so small, and the assay so poor, that the constant remark of the Cornish captains who accompanied me was that there must have been something got out of the mine which they could not see, or else it could never have paid. Besides this, the country was barren, and there were often many other local disadvantages. Still, however, it was evident to me that these mines somehow or other *must* have paid, or else they would not have been worked; and in spite of the disadvantages which were *before my eyes*, the natural conclusion was, that if they had once paid, they might surely pay again.

However, as soon as I afterwards saw a few of the miners at work, the problem was solved.

The miners who are now in Chile, though toiling in the path of their early days, have probably relaxed a little from the discipline of the Spaniards; but the extraordinary manner in which they still work, or rather slave, is almost incredible. The contrast between their lives and the ease and independence of the rest of the inhabitants of the country naturally leads the mind to reflect on the sad history of the South American mines; and this history, in my humble opinion, sufficiently accounts for, first, the impossibility which now exists of getting more miners; and, second, for the important truths, that the American mines have positively fallen in value since the country has been free, because the contents or produce of the mines are still the same, while the value of labor, &c., has necessarily increased; and therefore that, far from being able to get a *greater* profit from these mines than was extracted by the Spaniards, it would be impossible now to draw from them what they formerly repaid, and that many of them must continue deserted, for the evident reason that poor mines, as well as poor land, may be made productive by a system of cruelty and tyranny, when under a free government they must lie inactive and barren.

XVI

Conclusion

Having now completed a very rough and defective sketch of the pampas, &c., and some of the provinces of the Río Plata and of the governments and habits of the people, it is natural to consider how powerful this country must necessarily become, when, animated by a large population, enriched by the industry and intelligence of man, and protected by the integrity and power of well-constituted governments, it takes that rank in the civilized world which is due to its climate and soil; and as, in nature's great system of succession, "nations and empires rise and fall, flourish and decay," it is possible that this country, availing itself of the experience of past ages, may become the theater of nobler actions than any of the nations of the Old World, whose obscure march towards civilization was without a precedent to guide them, or a beacon to warn them of their dangers. And far from being jealous of the superior strength and energy which a young country may attain, it is pleasing to anticipate the prosperity which may await it, and to indulge a hope that its young arm may assert the dignity and the honor of human nature; that it may liberate the slave, and against every threat or danger support freedom, when the infirmities of an *older nation* may have rendered her incapable of the task.

But between this moral and political eminence which the pampas and the provinces of Río Plata may attain, and their present state, there is a distance which is evident to everyone, though no man can calculate the time which will be requisite to pass it. The difficulties to be encountered must necessarily be great, and it is not an improper or a useless subject of speculation to consider what some of these difficulties may be.

The great desideratum of these countries is population; for until there is a certain proportion of inhabitants, the provisions of life must necessarily be easily obtained, and people will remain indolent until necessity drives them to exertion. The overplus population of the Old World will undoubtedly flow towards these countries, bringing with it different habits, languages, and customs. The points at which the emigrants settle will depend upon the produce which they are best fitted for obtaining, and the governments of the different provinces must become more or less powerful in proportion to the success of these people. Some will rapidly rise, while others will be left for some time in the wretched state of poverty and inactivity in which they now exist; and the laws and regulations which govern the one will be insufficient, inapplicable, or contrary to the interests of the others. As the provinces become more vigorous, it will probably be found that the situations of many of the present capitals must unavoidably be changed. For instance, the maritime province of Buenos Aires already requires a harbor; and it is easy to foresee, that when commerce establishes its residence at the new port, the government must follow.

The language, religion, habits, and occupations of the different provinces will of course be influenced and affected by the quantity of foreign settlers, and the laws must vary with the exigencies which require them. The provinces, as they become powerful, will naturally desire to be independent; and the possibility of their being all governed from Buenos Aires will rapidly diminish.

During these or similar events, the provinces of the Río Plata must necessarily be in a troubled and unsettled state. The national government, thwarted in its plans, deserted sometimes by one province, and sometimes opposed by another, must often, unavoidably, act contrary to the interests of those plans it may have suggested; while the provincial governments must often suddenly be overturned, be annihilated and remodeled, until prosperity has afforded to society the liberal principles of a good education, which, with time and experience, will at last constitute governments practically suited to the country.

If the state of the provinces of Río Plata has been correctly sketched, and if the above should be a fair statement of some of the probable difficulties which these provinces will experience in their progress towards civilization, there are two questions to be considered which are very material to the interests of many individuals in our country.

1st. Is it advisable for those who are in reduced circumstances in England to migrate to these provinces?

2nd. Is it prudent for those of large capital to embark their money there in any permanent establishment or speculation?

My humble opinion on these two important questions is shortly as follows:

A poor individual, or a poor family, or a congregation of poor families, coming from England to these provinces, will instantly be relieved from that part of their sufferings which proceeded from absolute want of food, for they will arrive at a place where coarse beef is cheap. Artisans will obtain good wages in the town of Buenos Aires; but as English peasants are not fitted to perform any part of the gaucho's labor, they will not receive from them more than their board.

Now, at Buenos Aires, artisans will find provisions very dear, and although they receive more money than in England, they will not be able to live there so well. The lodgings, which are always unfurnished, are shockingly dirty, filled with all sorts of vermin; and, after all, they are extremely dear. Beef is sold in such a mangled state that when the Cornish miners first arrived, they often returned from the butchers' carts without buying the meat, being unable to make up their minds to eat it. The fowls at Buenos Aires are also very bad, for they feed upon raw meat; occasionally I have seen them hopping out of the carcass of a dead horse; and we all fancied that the eggs tasted of beef. The pigs are also carnivorous. Raw beef is cheap, but fuel (the coals which are used come from Newcastle; and almost all the potatoes from Falmouth), pepper, salt, bread, water, &c., are all so exorbitantly dear that the meat when cooked positively becomes expensive; and every article of clothing is 80 per cent dearer than in England.

The society of the lower class of English and Irish at Buenos Aires is very bad, and their constitutions are evidently impaired by drinking, and by the heat of the climate, while their morals and characters are much degraded. Away from the religious and moral example of their own country, and out of sight of their own friends and relations, they rapidly sink into habits of carelessness and dissipation, which are but too evident to those who come fresh from England; and it is really too true, that all the British emigrants at Buenos Aires are sickly in their appearance, dirty in their dress, and disreputable in their behavior. A poor person with a young family should therefore pause before he brings them into such society; for it is surely better that his children, until they arrive at an age to work, should occasionally be in want in England, than that their constitutions should be impaired, and those principles ruined, which induce every religious and honest man in England to labor with cheerfulness, and to return from his work with a healthy body and a contented mind.

A single man may imagine that he is able to resist the effects of bad society; that he would enjoy the climate and freedom of the country, and by attention, save up a sum of money to return to England—but he would find many unexpected difficulties.

The principal one to a working man is the climate, which in summer is so dreadfully hot that his constitution is unable to stand against it, and with every inclination to work he finds that his strength fails him, and that he is overpowered by a debility before unknown to him. He would then wish himself back in England, and his absence from his friends, and being unable to work, would make him discontented with a life which hangs heavy upon his hands, and which becomes more cheerless, because, unless he has a large sum of money, to pay for his passage, he sees that he is unable to return.

The above observations are not altogether theoretical. I particularly observed the unexpected effect which the climate had upon many English companies, and upon a large body of our English miners, who were selected in Cornwall for their good behavior, and who arrived in the provinces with every inclination to maintain their character. They saw the degraded state of the English settlers at Buenos Aires, and of their own accord they kept clear of them; but the cheapness of the spirits, and the heat of the climate were inducements to them to drink, which they found it very difficult to resist. As soon as the heat set in, the men were exhausted, and complained of a "feebleness" that they had never felt before; and this was so great that many of the strongest of them preferred going without meat to the fatigue of going through the sun to fetch it. This imbecility had its natural effect upon their minds, and they expressed their dislike of a climate in which they could make no exertions, and by which they were even exhausted while lying down or sitting still; and as soon as I determined on sending them home, they all most joyfully gave up the lucrative advantages which had induced them to come to the country, and none of them would remain, although by their agreements they might each have claimed sixty pounds instead of a passage, and might instantly have made very good contracts with the other mining companies; but they were all anxious to return, and I heard several of them say to each other that they had sooner work their fingers to the stumps in England than be gentlemen at Buenos Aires.

(We had all sorts of English speculations in South America, some of which were really amusing. Besides many brother companies which I met with at Buenos Aires, I found a sister association of milkmaids. It had suddenly occurred to some of the younger sons of John Bull that as there were a number of beautiful cows in the United Provinces of Río de la Plata, a quantity of good pasture, and as the people of Buenos Aires had no butter to their bread, a churning company would answer admirably; and before the idea was many months old, a cargo of Scotch milkmaids were lying becalmed under the Line, on their passage to make butter at Buenos Aires. As they were panting and sighing [being from heavy rains unable to come on deck], Neptune as usual boarded the ship, and the sailors who were present say that his first observation was that he had never found so many passengers and so few beards to shave; however, when it was explained to him, that they were not Britannia's *sons*, but Jenny Bulls, who have no beards, the old god smiled and departed. The people at Buenos Aires were thunderstruck at the unexpected arrival of so many British milkmaids. However, private arrangements had been made, and they, therefore, had milk before it was generally known that they had cows. But the difficulties which they experienced were very great: instead of leaning their heads against patient domestic animals, they were introduced to a set of lawless wild creatures who looked so fierce that no young woman who ever sat upon a three-legged stool could dare to approach, much less to milk them! But the gauchos attacked the cows, tied their legs with strips of hide, and as soon they became quiet, the shops of Buenos Aires were literally full of butter. But now for the sad moral of the story: after the difficulties had been all conquered, it was discovered, first, that the butter would not keep!—and secondly, that somehow or other the gauchos and natives of Buenos Aires . . . liked oil better!!)

From the above circumstances, and many other observations which I endeavored to make on the situations of a few English emigrants I met with in the different provinces, I am convinced that those who have hitherto emigrated to this country, as well as those who deserted from General Whitelocke's army, have passed their days in disappointment and regret—that the constitution of every individual has been more or less impaired—that their religious principles have altogether been destroyed

—and I therefore would sincerely advise poor people, particularly those who have families, not to migrate to such hot latitudes, if they have the means of supporting themselves in England.

In reply to the second question, whether it is prudent to embark a large capital in any permanent establishment or speculation in this country?—the Spanish South Americans have certainly become independent of the government of Spain, and this has of course proceeded from their own positive strength, and from the imbecility of the Spanish government; but supposing it to have arisen from the first cause only, still it must be admitted that a young nation may be strong enough to gain its independence before it has education, wisdom, or experience enough to know what to do with it; and taking into consideration the peculiar political situation of the country, I must own it appears to me that during the troubles and vicissitudes which must unavoidably attend the progress of these provinces towards civilization, it would be imprudent for a stranger to enter into any permanent establishment; for, ignorant of what is to happen, all he can depend upon is, that great changes will take place, that *he* must always be a responsible person, while unlooked-for revolutions may cause the governments or the individuals with whom he has established himself to vanish, leaving him in the wide plain without a remedy, and perhaps even without a just cause of complaint. He may have treated with a government which has ceased to exist, or with an individual whose fortune or whose influence may have suddenly disappeared, and be like the person who came from England to Buenos Aires some years ago under the promise that he should have a lucrative situation in the cabildo, and who learnt on his arrival that the cabildo had just been destroyed.

I can speak from my own private experience, for I was very nearly in a similar or a worse situation. I was furnished with letters of introduction to the governor of San Juan, and a copy of the then famous Carta de Mayo,

which had been published in that province to insure to us
religious toleration; but had I not fortunately been delayed upon my road, I should upon my arrival at San
Juan have been instantly thrown into prison with the
governor who was already confined, and from the window
of my dungeon I should have seen the public executioner
burning the Carta de Mayo, amidst the acclamations of
the people. Yet I could not have complained, for my
letters of introduction and the copy of the Carta de Mayo
had been sent to me with the best intention—and the
governor at San Juan had wished to give me a polite
reception; but the event was a political tempest which
had not been foretold.

The failure of the Rio Plata Mining Association is a
serious proof of the insufficiency of the governments of
La Plata. This public association was formed in London
in virtue of a decree, &c., from the government of Buenos
Aires, authorizing the formation of a company to work
the mines of the United Provinces, at the discretionary
choice of the company; and to promote this object, reports
were forwarded from the governors of the mining provinces describing their mines. Yet, on my arrival at Buenos
Aires, I found that almost the whole of the mines were
already sold by the governments to the opposition companies, and that the government of Buenos Aires, as well
as the governors of the provinces, had been totally unable
to fulfil the decree. Private interest and private speculators
had overpowered their act and their intention, and they
had only to confess—

TEMPORA MUTANTUR, ET NOS MUTAMUR IN ILLIS.